JJ FROST

Light Between the Shadows

Reflections on life

Matador
9 Priory Business Park
Kibworth Beauchamp
Leicestershire LE8 0RX, UK
Tel: (+44) 116 279 2299
Fax: (+44) 116 279 2277
Email: books@troubador.co.uk
Web: www.troubador.co.uk/matador

ISBN 978 1780885 476

British Library Cataloguing in Publication Data.
A catalogue record for this book is available from the British Library.

Typeset in Aldine401 BT Roman by Troubador Publishing Ltd
Printed and bound in the UK by TJ International, Padstow, Cornwall

Matador is an imprint of Troubador Publishing Ltd

This book is dedicated to Jenson, Bonnie and Darcey.

Our dear departed doggies passed away in 2010. Their love and devotion helped to inspire me on a daily basis. Sadly, within a period of five months, one by one we lost our wonderful trio. I pray they are happy together in heaven, and we will see them all again one day.

Acknowledgements

I would like to offer my gratitude to my dear, patient and caring husband David, who has helped me with his wisdom when writing this book. Also, a big thank you to the rest of my family and to my friends who have supported me over the years, and to those who have been kind enough to assist with the artwork and editing process.

As the years have pass, I am grateful for having been given the opportunity to meet so many wonderful people. Some have continued being part of my life, others have entered, stayed for a while and then we have gone our separate ways. Countless numbers of people have inspired me along my journey with their kindness, love and perception. Others have had a negative influence on my life with their selfishness and thoughtlessness, but still I have learnt from these experiences. Life has thrown what appear to be almost impossible challenges at times. Some events are not always going to be wholesome as our journeys take us on many uphill struggles. However, my life's challenges have certainly moulded me into the person I am today and for that I am truly grateful.

Contents

Introduction

'Light Between the Shadows' has been written with warmth and meaning; to open your heart, comfort your mind and heal your soul, when clarity and guidance are needed. There are times when our normal happy lives begin to tumble, and the deepest depth of despair is in sight. Without realising it, you may have chosen a route that has taken you along a path full of anguish and despair. Before you know it, the resulting outcome of events has knocked you sideways. It isn't until you recognise this is not your intended direction in life and head back onto your destined path, that life becomes balanced once again.
I hope and pray, this little book will be your guide and companion. To support you until the light begins to shine once more and rise up above the darkened shadows. These words are composed for you with kindness and grace; embrace their gentleness to help guide you along your onward journey. I hope and pray my inspired words will help you in times of need; to glide you over any uneven bumps that may present themselves along your destined path. If these thought provoking verses help heal your wounds, then my job is done. Let us enjoy the peaceful moments, embrace the fun and laughter, and accept the times of sorrow and sadness, as there will always be shadows where there is light.

Bless you all........

Abuse

Are you an unfortunate soul who is in the habit of seeking out an abuser? Is the desire so strong you need to step back into your comfort zone and continue this miserable cycle just because it is how your life has been for so long? Are the signs so obvious if someone has been abused or have they the ability to hide it well from others?

The abuse will devour your soul, slowly, slowly, slowly eat away, with the power and strength of an ox, not willing to give in, the pain spreads to every part of you, every hair on your body can tell the same story and does not ease as time goes by.

Abuse is like a merry-go-round, a continuing cycle, going on and on. The pattern of an abuser can be familiar to many; the anger builds, often rapidly, then the sparks begin to fly, the temper explodes uncontrollably and continues until boiling point is reached. The mental, sometime physical, abuse begins; it turns into rage and continues until eventually exhaustion takes over and calm returns once more. But still the victim is on edge and watches the abuser's every move, carefully choosing their words so as not to fuel the fire, smouldering inside. After a while the sorrow begins and they may apologise for their actions. Some beg forgiveness while others simply blame the victim, as it must be their fault for provoking their rage and anger. Often this is followed by the promise that it will never happen again, they have learnt their lesson.

Calm then steps in and good behaviour begins once more, so the abuser feels justified to brush it all under the carpet and pretend it never happened. As the wheel continues to rotate round and around so does the abuse; enjoy the peace while it lasts as the pattern will repeat itself soon.

The only way to stop this wheel of abuse is to jam something in the spokes. Sparks may fly to begin with, but the wheels will begin to slow down until you regain control and eventually it will grind to a halt. The weeks ahead will be tough, but don't be tempted to return to the abusive relationship. Be patient; gradually you will begin to find the peace and harmony you deserve and desperately desire. It will all be worth it.

(abuse photo) by anibro

Addiction Conceals my Pain

Why is my addiction so powerful? The immense control my addiction has is terrifying; I cannot break free from the mighty grasp. I try to escape but the urge is so strong and I am not in control anymore. Do you have an addiction?

Are you someone who enjoys alcohol, or drugs; shopping or gambling? My desire would be to dive head first into a magical pool of heavenly warm silky smooth chocolate, and just wallow there for an hour or two.

The desperate emotion is numbed for a short period of time and a veil of satisfaction temporarily melts away my tension. But soon the desire to receive my fix will return, it is so powerful how can I resist the temptation?

Why can I not get the same buzz from just doing a good deed, surely this gift far outweighs the obsession I have. But I feel passionate about my addiction, I long to get my fix to satisfy my desire. I wake every morning and can't wait to ease my desperate cravings. To live this way is certainly not the easy road, but it is the road I have chosen to take for myself. If it were easy I wouldn't feel so desperate all the time, and depressed for being so weak willed. I weep for a moment while I wait to see if my willpower will appear.

When I am far away from my fix, my body starts to quiver, my mind races like a high-speed train. I cannot seem to slow down enough to find a peaceful moment.

I don't want to be controlled anymore, I want to open the door to freedom, and allow the rays of sunshine to engulf me and dissolve the dark stormy cloud that has dampened my every waking hour. I want help. Please will you help me, care for me, comfort me; give me strength and above all be my friend.

(cake addiction photo) - by ukanda
(cigarette addiction photo) - by sbumu

Affairs of the Heart

I am tangled in a web I find impossible to unravel. My innocence is apparent when another becomes woven in and the web becomes completely knotted. Uncontrolled rage breaks loose and the feeling of being violated is so prominent and painful. How could they be so cruel?

I am told 'nothing has happened.' Does that make everything OK? The intimate words that would have been spoken between the two feel worse than the knowledge of my partner sharing a bed with another.

The lies, the deceit, devour my entire body and soul, and slowly rot through to the pit of my stomach. The emotions I have discovered are so painful. Will I begin the rollercoaster ride as a victim of the affair? Or will the initial shock turn into anger and hatred, betrayal and bewilderment?

Then, bitterness and jealousy may show their ugly heads, or perhaps it is the sinking realisation that I am on my own again. Will this bring out emotions like denial or guilt as surely it must be my fault my partner had an affair?

As time passes, strong, sometimes unhealthy emotions appear and often progress and eat their way into the depths of my soul. It would take a miracle to shift them as the hurt has gone beyond help. But who is suffering? Do I honestly think my hard new exterior is having any affect on my ex? My acid tongue is only making me suffer.

I have to continually look in the mirror at the bitter and twisted casualty I have become. I am the only one who is sad and angry, my partner in the meantime is having a fantastic time with the new love of their life.

From tomorrow, I must leave all the decaying, rotten emotions behind; close the door and make sure it is well and truly bolted. If I choose not to, the only one who is suffering is me.

(affairs of the heart photo) - by transcript

Angel – my Invisible Caretaker

Do you have a guardian angel?

Should I talk to my guardian angel? Do I truly believe I have one? How do I reach a resolve when I am alone and a decision has to be made; where did the decision come from? Did I honestly find it all by myself? Why have I not thought of it before?

Do you have a guardian angel?

Why is it sometimes after a good night's sleep I have found the answer to a problem that may have been hounding me for days.

Do you have a guardian angel?

The nagging feeling inside that is warning me of a potential threat - could this be my angel trying to guide me away from this path as it is heading for trouble?

Do you have a guardian angel?

What about those uncomfortable innermost thoughts that are telling me someone close to me is an unhealthy influence and can easily drain every ounce of life from me. Somehow, someway, I find the strength to prise myself away, dropping them from my social network. Where does my strength come from when, for so long, I have been suffering their behaviour; they have sucked the life from me? Then out of the blue I am able to walk away, close the door and bolt it firmly behind me. Where did my strength come from?

Do you have a guardian angel?

I must have a guardian angel as I know when I am alone I am not really alone. I may not have any human companions around but I still feel harmonious and comfortable; enveloped by a warm loving sensation. This inner feeling is letting me know my wonderful loyal angel is close by. Have faith and trust your inner most thoughts.

Do you have a guardian angel?

(angel photo) - by ell brow

Anger – Next Stop the Shredder

Anger is akin to cancer, it can spread through your body and linger, not wanting to surrender until eventually it engulfs every last speck of peace you once had.

As a caterpillar engulfs a cabbage, cancer eats away like the caterpillar. Once it has greedily eaten its way through one leaf it moves on to the next. Anger can spread like the cancer until every part of your body is filled with it.

The rage can be controlled, if you try hard enough. Don't let it be in command of you; it can often make you hysterical, as it comes from the deepest part of your soul.

It must be within your control, or does something or somebody else steer you through your life?

I can see your anger by the look on your face; your expression says it all. Your body language shows the fire is smouldering within and can ignite at any moment.

Rarely does a physical altercation occur without the prior expression of your rage. Anger is a normal emotion and not in itself a problem; it is your response to anger that determines whether or not others should be concerned.

How do you release your anger? Does it take over your world? Does it ruin each day with uncontrollable thoughts drifting back to the unhappy experience that sparked you in the first place?

Will you become bitter and blame others for your deep-rooted pain and anguish? What if you don't release your anger? It surely turns inwards, making you feel desperate and stressed.

Does your anger stay with you, not wanting to leave your side, reinforced by a negative interpretation of things that surround you? It is always just beneath the surface ready to explode at a moment's notice.

Why not break the cycle, release the anger, and free yourself from this torment. You have the right to be at peace and abandon this wicked emotion.

Freedom is within your reach, take a hold and hang on tight. Slowly peel away your angry thoughts, layer by layer, deal with the fallout, and release your emotion until you feel it subside. Visualise it being put through a shredder; it will be so finely cut it can no longer be deciphered, so freeing you from future torment.

Peace, be with you always.

Animal Kingdom

Our wonderful kingdom of animals is a blessing and a gift from our divine creator. Some are adored by us and live in harmony in our homes; some are abused by us. Some serve a valuable purpose to help us in our daily lives. A guide dog will lead as there is no light to see. Some help us herd our sheep, whilst others can warn us of danger lurking in the shadows. What a beautiful gift they are. Their unconditional love is so precious and valued by many. Their purity is untouched by any form of evil, they must surely be angels sent from heaven.

We have an extraordinary bond with our loyal companions; they are uncontaminated in their intentions just wanting to love and serve us. It is our interference that has made some, without cause, aggressive. We strive to breed the perfect fighting machine to satisfy the evil streak some people have to watch dogs fight till the death.

While other people like to play God and manipulate animal genes to create a variety of shapes and sizes to suit our desires. Some like to make the dogs nose squashed in like a pancake, or make their bodies longer, legs shorter, or even make them small enough to fit into your coat pocket.

Please forgive our selfishness; for they are with us on loan; we don't own them and they have the right to be treated well. So if they live alongside you, keep them safe and warm, feed them well, it is a small request they ask in return.

Be kind and gentle and they will show you utter devotion and extreme loyalty; they will always be by your side. Cherish these feelings, nurture their love, embrace and enjoy every moment. This wonderful gift is free, but the wealth you will receive is priceless.

If you use an animal for food, be kind enough to let their spirit leave their body in a dignified way, you are then welcome to take their remains. The body is merely a vessel to carry their spirit around, so take it with pleasure once their spirit has gone, as their work on earth is done.

(animal kingdom - pig photo) - by maxwell hamilton

Battle of the Bulge

With each passing year I seem to be becoming more and more podgy. These chubby rolls seem to increase in size each time I see my naked reflection. To some, an extra spare tyre around the middle is just part of life, to others it's a sign of gluttony, to me it is ghastly.

I weep when I catch a glimpse of myself in a shop window as I walk on by. My gruesome appearance must be revolting to others, how can anyone still want to be my friend?

I know I have to live with what I have been given, my height, my stature, but surely I should be in control of the blubber surrounding me, that never leaves me, just clings to me like glue.

I have been blinkered. I never noticed my increase in body mass. Where did it come from? Before I knew it my clothes just became tighter. I thought the zips were just becoming rusty, as they were so stiff and difficult to do up.

Now here I am, desperate for a return of the time when I can bend forwards without rolls of blubber appearing around my middle.

I am now turning to naughty food for comfort; I often have episodes of compulsive eating, desperate to fill my face with as much junk as possible which I mistakenly think helps with my depression. Sadly all it does is make me feel worse?

Am I eating because I'm hungry or are my emotions clouding my judgment whilst, my depressive mind is taking control?

Is it worth depriving my body of forbidden foods if it makes me miserable? I must just take control of my urges, allowing myself small amounts of forbidden food. That way my body will be more at ease in allowing me to enjoy a healthy nutritious diet.

From this moment forward, I have control and I will win this battle. Hold on tight to this positive feeling as it will aid me along the path to a wonderfully contented happy me.

Beauty Beneath the Shell

How do you view beauty? Perhaps the rays of the sun slowly gliding over a meadow displaying glistening bluebells, on a beautiful early spring morning? The birds adding to the splendour, singing sweetly in the trees nearby, most would agree this is beauty at its best.

When it comes to us as humans how do we define beauty? Is it someone who catches your eye, you can't stop looking their way; someone you continually talk about to anyone who will listen. Surely we are all created for a reason and have a purpose so that makes us all beautiful, doesn't it? Do you stand in front of a mirror and admire your reflection or cringe at the person staring back at you. But wait, you are only looking at the physical beauty; what about the beauty within, isn't this more important and what we should be concentrating on?

Not often are we complimented on our inner beauty, only measured instead by our external good looks. Everyone is unique, beauty is gracious, a sparkle in the eyes, a warm welcoming smile; beauty is what you exude so keep the essence of what makes you one of a kind. Remember you are one of our creator's children through whose eyes we are all beautiful.

You cannot compare yourself to a catwalk model or pictures of beautifully flawless airbrushed women as portrayed in celebrity magazines. Be happy with the shell you have been given as you cannot change it; you may be able to tweak certain areas but the basic structure must remain the same.

It is more important to change the inner person. Rid yourself of all negativity; stop your harsh tongue from upsetting others and enjoy the rewards of doing good rather than living your life in a self-centred way; the benefits will be so worthwhile.

From tomorrow, be content, be joyful, and above all be happy and at peace.

(beauty beneath the shell photo) by - fifth world art

Born Alone - to Live - to Die Alone

I am surrounded by people, my address book is full, but I never have enough time to spend with my friends and family. Is this why I feel so alone? That surely doesn't make sense. I take a moment to ponder; do I need time to at least look more deeply at my life? Yes I have my family, and yes my friends, but ultimately the direction I take is my choice. I may be influenced by others but do I listen to their good advice or follow a path that could take me along a sticky track with obstacles along the way? This makes me feel lonely. I want to be loved and I want to feel needed. I want to feel like my life has meaning. If I were not here then surely I would be missed or am I just another piece in life's jigsaw? But wait; a jigsaw is not complete without all the pieces so I must be just as important as everyone else. I am here for a reason; I know I have a purpose I just wish I knew what.

Where do I go when I take my last breath? My human body has ceased to work, it cannot function anymore, but does my spirit find a new path and continue on its journey? Oh I do hope so; otherwise it would all seem so pointless.

I wait to learn of my chosen destiny? I must be patient, and then all will be revealed.

So for now I will accept I was born alone. I will live my life and accept the times of struggle and make the most of, and enjoy, the peaceful times.

Ultimately I will die alone as we all do in reality; this is my last moment, the only one left for me now. I cherish it with grace, and am peaceful in my last moment here.

My new moments will begin, shortly.

Box of Troubles

Why does life have to have its ups and downs? I know I should accept that this pattern is normal and not be disappointed when life takes a downward spiral as it just has to on occasions. What if I could find a way to alter life's pattern to suit my desires? Surely this would make life more enjoyable? I can't worry about the consequences, not today at least, I'm sure it will all work out fine.

I know some are fearful that if they open the box it will only bring trouble, a little like the warning on Pandora's Box. The casket is closed for a reason, and this must be obeyed. Once the box is opened I am told I must be prepared to deal with a whole host of troubles. I am not superstitious so this does not concern me. My curiosity and desire is strong; I must open the box, it is bewitching and tempting. I cannot say no, the urge is so appealing. I cannot control my desire, and so I open the box..... it is only as I raise the lid that I notice the written warnings on the side, the seven deadly sins. They appear attractive at first, what is there to fear? I then realise the box is full of sin; it can destroy all faith, hope and goodness from within. The voices inside the box will try to persuade others like me to keep the box open. If you stumble across the box, however much you feel an uncontrollable attraction, beware; life will never be the same again, if you open it.

Sadly my warnings were ignored and the box has taken control of its next victim. The rays of the beautiful warm sunshine, once again slowly disappear and eventually day turns into a grey and murky long night; the gentle summer breeze turns into a cold raging winter's storm. Any happy emotions change to wicked devious thoughts. The more evil that is unleashed, the more damp and dark the world becomes. All I can feel around me is deep gloom and despondency; the devil will engulf us all. Oh why did I fall to temptation? Why could I not find the strength to prevent you from opening the box? Where do we find the power to close the box? Can anybody help us? I do not think I have the mighty force needed to close it on my own. The devil has such a powerful hold I feel I am almost drowning in misery.

Please help, for evil will prevail if we let it. Act now before it is too late, let not the future be only a distant memory.

Bull or Hedgehog

Where do I fit into the social structure? If I were an animal would people compare me to a bull or a hedgehog, or could I fall into both categories depending on the situation. When confronted with a difficult situation do I go charging ahead, not worrying who is in my path, or do I crawl into my defensive ball? Slithering away to retreat into a corner, so I can raise my protective shield of piercing spikes? I wonder which is worst to be confronted with? The Bull who steams ahead, bulldozing anyone or anything on its route, sometimes not stopping to take a breath or even to apologise for their possibly aggressive manner? Or the Hedgehog who will back-away from possible confrontation and recoil, hoping to disappear into the ether. Sadly this just allows frustrations to fester, becoming stale and rancid, eating away inside until they reach the deepest part of one's soul; growing and growing until they devour your entire spiritual body. Outwardly the spikes are now in full bloom and can pierce their victim without any warning, which can be just as painful as the bull's horns.

So which way is the easiest to handle, or are they just as difficult as each other? Who am I, the bull or the hedgehog?

Can I change my ways, now I know how painful my words can be? Can any of us change or should we accept and enjoy our differences? After all if we had the same views on everything, life would become very dull and boring.

My partner is the opposite of me; I shouldn't fight it, but try and admire the different views and not concentrate on the traits that can be exasperating. I must view the differences as complementary and keep the extreme emotional differences to a healthy minimum.

Remember, love governs all so I should never let a difference of opinion linger; the finale should be with love at the centre, and, more importantly, a sense of humour close to hand.

(bull photo) by - beezum
(hedgehog photo) by- xshamethestrongx

Bum Magnet

Am I living with a low life bum, a dozy individual who still acts like a child of twelve and has never left his mummy's side. This out of work sloth spends more time with his X-Box than he does with me. Am I falling into the same trap as before? Is my current boyfriend turning into a loser like the last one and the one before that?

He was my idol, my hero; I placed him on a pedestal. He is a good person, I'm sure he is, I know he doesn't mean to drag me down and treat me like dirt, it's just his way.

We sit together and spend hour after hour talking. This time he has vowed to change, to grow up and be a man. Afterwards we kiss and make up, but I wonder, am I a jerk to believe him as I have heard these empty promises before? Can he change or will I be back in the same position in a couple of weeks,
full of despair and frustration as I realise he has let me down again? My friends say 'kick him to the kerb, then surround yourself with people you feel comfortable with, who give you confidence, understanding and love you for just being you'.

I am blessed to be given life, so I should live it to the full and not waste it on low life characters.

I have been given a key to open a door to happiness, if only I knew how to find the lock to release it.

If I had my time again, would I choose this man? Sadly, before I knew it, his charm crept under my skin and now it's hard to prise him away. I worry if I stay with him my life will pass me by.

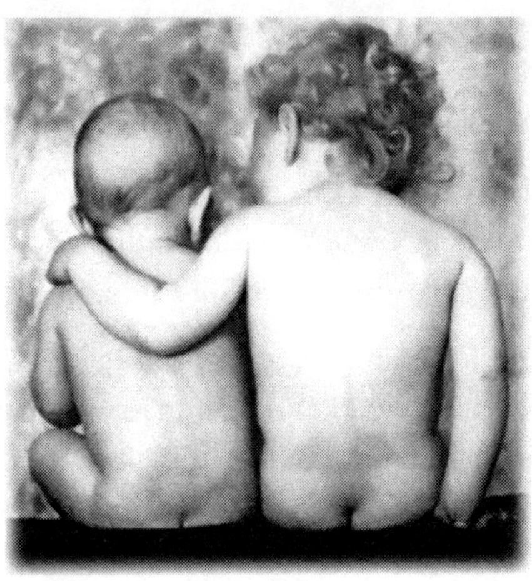

A time to think, a time to contemplate; but no time for revenge. Do I stay or should I go? If I go, will I learn from this mistake?

Will I hold on to these unhealthy feelings, unable to forgive him and keeping him prisoner in my mind? Will I keep him locked in my subconscious, caged like a wild animal constantly fighting to get out?

Will this give me pleasure or will the price I pay to keep him captive be poisonous and contaminate me?

(bum magnet photo) - by victor babbick

Celebrity Idol

We admire them from afar. Perhaps your idol is a famous person who is a character actor in a theatre play, a movie hero or heroine, or a soap opera star.

Their acting is so convincing; I know I begin to believe in their character so they must be real. I am mesmerised, admiring their personality, even wanting to be like them. I change my appearance so I can look and act as they do. I restyle my hair and change my clothes. This will surely make my life as exciting and filled with nonstop parties and dinner invitations as theirs. Then I see a transformed view as the cameras are turned away and their true personality shines through. It is now I realise my idol is not the person I thought I knew. Where has that gentle sweet individual gone? How can I hide the enormous disappointment I feel? My hero has let me down; they have shown their inner self and it isn't very attractive, in fact all I see now is an ogre. This person cares little for others and disrespects anyone who doesn't hold an A-list celebrity members badge. In a superstar world, many are self-absorbed, manipulative, and extremely vain. Their arrogance is draining to all around them. The groupies who tag along with these celebrities, catering to their every desire, only increase the celebrity's self-importance. The paparazzi add to their pompous manner, constantly hounding them to get the juicy gossip.

I think it is they who should envy me. My life is peaceful and I am content in my own skin; it may not be perfect but it serves the purpose while I am here. As long as my bodily shell works, and my mind is content, then I have the greatest gift of all....Peace.

Childhood - a Lifetime to Remember

Are my struggles a consequence of my childhood? Do I believe all my memories are happy ones, or have I blocked out the unhappy times and troubles? Would people have seen me as a sad and gloomy child, never wanting to mix with other children perhaps for fear of rejection? My past experiences must have affected my behaviour and ability to deal with day-to-day ups and downs, otherwise I would not be burdened with these whirling thoughts.

Many people blame an unhappy childhood if a depressing weight pulls them down, never wanting to be alone for long periods before those decaying thoughts return.

I know these experiences have affected my life; do I want the remainder of my days to continue in this way? The resentment I am carrying just brings more sorrow and woe. I must not ruin the remainder of my time and all who share in my life. I must not carry any bitterness however much it hurts; it is not a family trait that should be encouraged and it certainly isn't a trait to be proud of. I must not continue the cycle of these unhealthy feelings. I must not put the burden on my children and allow them carry it forward to the next generation.

I must realise this is my life and nobody else can live it. It is never too late to experience a happy childhood, I just have to find the combination to unlock those tightly knotted thoughts.

The rest of my life begins today. The path ahead I'm sure will be rough; it could even highlight some previously buried painful thoughts. I must press on it will be worth it. I must be strong and be patient, not expecting miracles; time will heal. Faith will carry me through.

(childhood photo) - by david castillo dominici

Chores - the Never Ending Battle

Some chores can be fun, some can be therapeutic, and then there are the ones that we all just dread. Some hate the task of matching up socks because there seems to be a mysterious vortex that sucks in just one sock always leaving a lonely unpaired one in the bottom of the wash basket. It is one of life's mysteries; will we ever find the matching sock?

If only I could feel that cleaning could become my new therapy, friend, or hobby, would I then enjoy my chores?

I set about my task to clean while the kids are at school. Once my goal is completed, I stand back and admire the gleaming worktops, the shiny sink, and the beautifully polished floor. Then I hear in the distance what can only be described as a herd of elephants racing up the garden path; the door is flung open and three mucky looking offspring come charging in. One by one they kick off their shoes, throw down their school rucksacks and head straight for the kitchen to raid the fridge like savages. Within a matter of minutes, my beautiful spotless home is turned into what looks like a warzone. They then swarm like angry bees to the living room, flick on the television and plant themselves on the sofa clutching crisp packets and chocolate bars; there they stay without a care in the world.

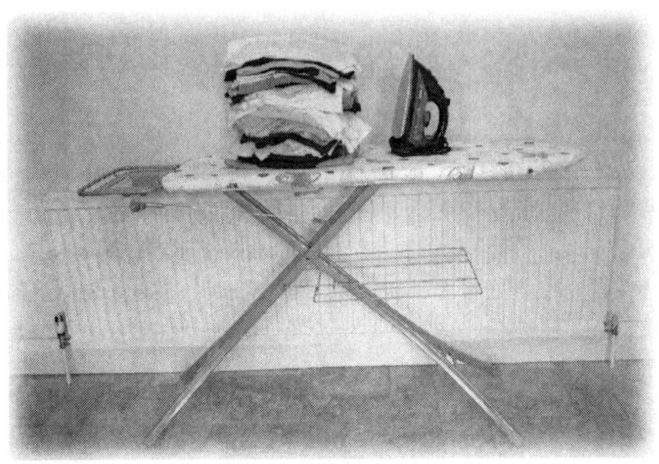

The sad part is I can't rebel. I can't say 'tools down' until I get help from other family members. Sadly the true fact of the matter is nobody else will step in to do the chores, and so the messy untidy house gets worse. When your friend or neighbours pop in unannounced they won't think badly of your husband or your kids, the only person they will judge for such a messy house is you.

Happy cleaning!

Coffee Break

A time to relax a time to reflect, is my time used wisely? I never realised the price I would pay for missing my coffee break. Another day passes by; again I missed my coffee break. Those important relaxing moments not taken again, I'll try again tomorrow.

A period of calm missed is another chance for the stress devil to creep in. His wicked grasp around you will gradually tighten; there is a strong likelihood he will seize any opportunity to force his control further, slowly but surely suffocating any remaining free will. I shout from the deepest seas and the tallest mountains: 'be on guard; keep strong'. If I feel my will is being tested it is time to take action, never let him win. His aim is to bring me down if he can. I am tired but I keep going. I'm sure after a good night's sleep I will feel better in the morning. I must not let my life become a brief episode in-between my daily work.

A new day begins and I fear I will have another missed coffee break. My time to relax has passed once again. I am just too busy to stop. Another day ends, my evening has vanished, wasted moments again, I am so exhausted all I can do is flop on the sofa and fall into a disturbed, dream filled sleep.

In the distance I hear the clock strike on the half hour. I open my eyes; it is now 12.30a.m. I wish I had gone to bed earlier, leaving the sofa I climb the stairs and crawl into my bed, too tired even to take off my makeup.

I lie there for a while thinking, tomorrow will be an easier day; I have a plan now, I will find time to relax, I deserve it. I cannot put off my tomorrow again. Sadly history has repeated itself. Today I forgot to take my coffee break, what will my excuse be tomorrow?

I awake, I am hurting, but why? I am not old, why has this pain woken me? What is happening? I can't move, I must call the doctor; oh no, not now, I promise I will take time to relax. I wish I had listened to my inner voice. I should have slowed down, and now my heart is poorly; why did I not listen? I do hope it is not too late. As I drift away into a preoccupied sleep my last thoughts are: 'perhaps I will stop for my coffee break today!'

Composure is Bliss

Am I a person with absolute composure, exuding a calm manner, a tranquil state of mind? A person who looks as though they are gliding as they walk, portraying a confident personality? Would you class me as a balanced, unflappable, nonchalant person I wonder? Could I show this as my exterior while inside, I am in utter chaos?

How does one hold on to this facade, not wishing for anyone to experience the real me? I am battling and fighting a war inside; this agonising inner conflict never ceases. Why can I not settle? I'm sure if I had internal composure the conflict would cease. How do some people control their emotions in stressful situations and keep their composure? The inner strength they possess must be wonderful. How can I remain calm when someone is so spiteful? They have wounded me so deeply with such hurtful words. To extinguish these burning flames is almost impossible for they continue to smoulder. If only I had the ability to self-regulate my emotions; not panicking every time I am faced with a threat or a stressful situation. I'm sure my life would be easier.

Strong leaders always appear calm and unruffled, demonstrating their control while portraying a positive attitude.

I must not allow the 'fight or flight' message in my mind to take control then I won't act first and think about my irrational actions later.

I must control my strong emotions and behave in a rational manner in difficult situations; keeping my composure at all times. I will be strong and do all I can to regain my self-control.

I'll keep my compass pointing north and eventually good will shine through as my journey ahead continues.

(composure photo) - by deneyterrio

Confidence can Crumble

My life is filled with many obstacles; most which I seem to collide into. Oh how it shakes my confidence. Why is it so many come my way? They seek me out, trip me up and bleed me dry.

My confidence is weak; I struggle to find even a single smile for each new day. I wish I could accept who I am and not listen to the depressing influences around me. I yearn to just accept myself for who I am, as this is the only person I can be. All other bodies around me are taken and have souls inside. Mine is the only one left so I ought to enjoy it. Keeping my shell in good condition, my posture should be upright; otherwise I am admitting to others how gloomy I feel and how my life is one huge struggle. I have to trust my inner voice to guide me through each day; it is hard to continually stay positive as my destructive thoughts are desperate to surface. They grow and gain strength and before I realise it they have overtaken all my positive thoughts. I must not be fooled; they do not like me, they do not support me; all they want to do is try and suppress me. I must fight with every muscle I own to break down the negativity.

I must try not to dwell on the sad memories I hold within. The unhappy emotion brings moisture to settle in my eyes and my body begins to crumble. I feel so fragile I feel so hopeless inside. My confidence is becoming less and less.

The good times always make me feel so much happier and content. If I do recall sad memories I should imagine myself as a spectator instead of the participant, viewing the scene from the wings. Visualise standing behind the negative me, mentally pushing this person away, until the vision is completely banished from sight.

For today, I will stand tall, smile a little smile and be thankful I am alive and free to live life to the full.

(confidence photo) - by bang_in_there

Conquer the Divide
Good Versus Evil

Who classes evil as good and darkness a blessing? Who hungers bitterness to triumph over sweet. Some will trick you into thinking they are harmless lambs only to one day reveal themselves as ferocious wolves; they will rip you apart as soon as your back is turned.

The struggle between good and evil is never ending. Evil is greedy for more hardship and suffering, never wanting to ease the pressure, craving more and more endless pain.

Beware, when the balance shifts and the demonic power increases; all the good and positive forces become stunned and overwhelmed. Around every corner evil is lurking, trying to stop the seekers of peace from practicing. The evil forces recruit vulnerable anti-social people, applaud chaotic insane behaviour, and enjoy dark energies, waging war on anyone who crosses their path.

It is impossible to annihilate them completely, the only hope is to loosen the grasp so good can seep through and penetrate their shield.

Hold on to the knowledge there is a greater power ready to stand by to give you support and a comforting helping hand when the need arises. Our health may suffer, the earth may appear like it is bleeding from within, and our spirit may weaken, but good must fight back with full force to regain control.

Extinguish once again the demonic hold, the excessive indulgence, the inappropriate use of authority. For now, we have to live with the on-going shift of power between good and evil. There will always be conflict as the battle continues.

Fear not, a little way ahead is light, the turning point for mankind. When we win the physical battle, give yourself time, enjoy adjusting to the new wonderful golden age ahead, as tranquillity will be within your grasp and remain for eternity.

(conquer the divide photo) – by randy son of robert

Dangerous World

I look around and everyone I meet is fighting their own daily battles, treading on eggshells, as the world is full of danger. I know the world is filled with wickedness, but what am I doing to make a difference? Am I just waiting for someone else to transform the earth to become the harmonious world we all wish for? If I am not satisfied with the way the world is heading then I should be prepared to help make some changes.

In the holy Bible our divine creator calls us to be utterly ruthless in our lives. He tells us not to compromise with the dark side, otherwise evil will ensnare us and become a thorn in our side. If we let it penetrate deep within it will consume our whole being. The devil will lay a trap at every opportunity to lure us towards his sinful ways. Oh yes it may be tempting, but don't be fooled by his persuasive methods. Once he has taken a hold no longer will you smile; each day you will wish to be your last. All thoughts and actions are negative, the clouds loom and darkness falls; you wait for the sunrise and it never comes. Each step we take, each corner we turn, we are confronted with sadness and despair.

If you sense evil is lurking in the shadows, keep away. If you are low and vulnerable the devil won't demand you walk along his path, he will gently persuade you, agreeing with you, saying nothing is your fault, it is others that are wrong. He will put doubt in your mind and so you begin to distrust all around you.

The devilish signs are not obvious; he is cunning and wants you all for himself. Many people have been tempted and fallen into the devil's grasp.

Don't be fooled by thinking if you follow his ways you will outwit everyone and never have to face our heavenly creator on your day of judgement.

Do you really want to take the chance and wait and see what the consequences will be? I think not.

Death is Not an Option

Death is neither good nor evil, it just is. Life only has meaning because there is an end. If you are affected by the loss of a loved one don't be angry with the angels of death as they stand in a neutral zone.

Death is inevitable; death is a part of life. Some view the loss of a loved one as a relief; their sadness has ended not because you have lost the person, but because their pain has ceased. The suffering is no more. Life for now is measured by consciousness. When the breath has stopped, death will follow, then there is a pause.

Give yourself time to reflect and be happy for the times you had together. Don't let the sadness linger, don't be scared. Hold this close to your heart and be at peace to face each day ahead.

If we can believe and trust what is written in scripture, one day we will meet again and live together for eternity. Keep this belief close to your heart and when the sadness falls, mentally surround yourself with these reassuring thoughts.

Imagine being wrapped in a beautiful, glowing, Golden Fleece filled with love, light and warmth; overflowing with harmony, peace and tranquillity. Have faith in knowing you are not alone; the extreme ache in your heart is being healed by a power beyond our comprehension.

When sadness falls, take a deep breath then slowly exhale, enjoy the relaxation this gives you, allow yourself time to adjust to the changes in circumstance.

Your departed loved one touched the earth and many lives along their path. Their time has come to an end and now for those who remain the grieving begins.

Nothing can prepare you for this heart wrenching feeling. Knowing how to swim is not enough as the raging waters of grief are overwhelming, sinking lower and lower in the waters of sorrow. It takes courage and strength that sometimes can only be found when you reach the bottom of the ocean. As the days follow the healing will begin. Then and only then can you slowly rise to the surface and find the glistening sea of calm.

One thing you know for sure, your pain cannot get any worse. It WILL get better; time is a great healer.

Devil in Disguise

Where are my spiritual thoughts coming from? Are they always from our heavenly father or could they be from someone else? Can I trust that our divine leader is always by my side, guiding me along the way, or could I be influenced by the darker side without realising it?

The devil is cunning and devious; he pretends to give good advice and help in times of need. I have to be careful, I don't want to confuse true loving guidance against the crafty ways of the devil. He can be manipulative and will try whatever he can to steer me towards his wicked ways. Once he takes a hold his contagious wickedness multiplies and spreads to every part of my body and soul.

Trust my inner voice; as I know the devil's way will never win. However much evil tries to fight and take over, good will shine through.

His wickedness will always be there waiting in the wings. I may be faced with many challenging uphill struggles and obstacles. I may have to deal with sorrow and grief, and times when stress reaches boiling point and my whole body feels like it could break and shatter into little pieces.

Ultimately, good will prevail and eventually triumph; history has shown this to be the case time and time again. Along the way many may dip their toes in the ways of the devil. They may dabble with drugs or alcohol, even violent irrational behaviour. The devil is making us more and more self-centred.

The first step to bring peace and harmony back into our lives is the hardest. You are not alone; many have been tempted. Together we can win the battle. Our communities need to regain the kindness and true friendship our ancestors used to enjoy. We are being given warning signs, if we choose to ignore these signs will the threat of Armageddon really come true as predicted?

The spiritual battle between good and the forces of evil will be drawn together. The appointed Messiah will lead us forward to banish materialism, promiscuity, and all hardship that is around us on earth.

Let it not be too late for you. To disregard the warning could be a mistake you may not even want to consider.

(devil in disguise photo) - by vancouver film school

Disease

The disease starts quietly; the absent fanfare is apparent. No pain is felt, no discomfort, just stillness. Where are the signs or symptoms? I feel at ease so how can I be affected by disease.

Is the cause from an organ malfunction, or is my disease rooted in a troubled state of mind? I know it is unfair to have this worry but why me? Then again, why not? Is it really luck of the draw, have I just picked the short straw?

I was given life so to waste it on worrying is pointless. I will have fun while I can and smile each and every day. I feel strong today so I must share my worries. Tomorrow may come and I may not feel so powerful; talking may be difficult as dimly the light glows within, fading as the moments pass. Catch the brightness before it disappears.

If my disease began from my turbulent mind, did this make my blood vessels rage from resentment or the acid in my tummy bubble away from stress? Does my heart race with a never-ending deafening drumbeat because I am so impatient?

Please find where my anxiety lives in my body and banish it forever. I should pray and command the disease to leave my body and allow the healing to begin.

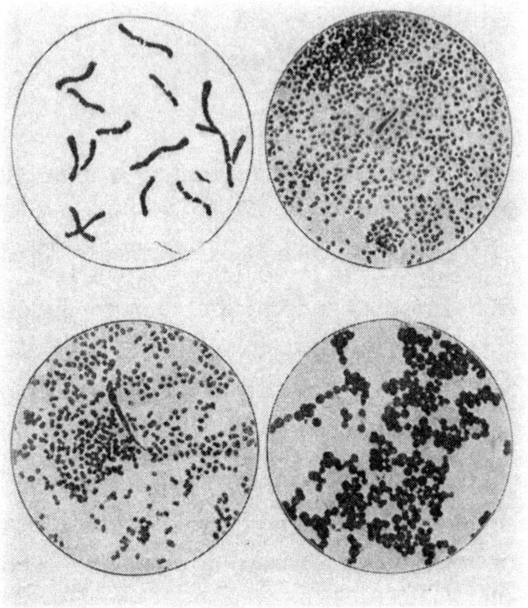

For now I have been given the gift of life, the power to take control, the ability to love and be loved. Speak of the pleasure of life, because death, for today, is not an option.

(disease photo) - by ephemeral scraps

Divine Guidance

Do I believe in the existence of a divine creator? Perhaps I see him as the ultimate evil for betraying me as he allows my loved ones to die.

Has God let me down and neglected me? Am I holding onto a belief which causes needless pain and anguish? Did I play judge and jury and find him guilty of 'His' actions before giving him a fair trial? Or do I view death as the final part of life and, because we have free will, death just is?

I was created, so I guess I should always be open to receiving divine guidance clearly and completely. We are not humans having a spiritual experience; we are spiritual beings having a human life. I find this hard to accept, as thinking of anything other than our planet and all that surround me can be rather daunting.

We are told God is there for all of us, he will help and guide us when we ask, but if the timing for help is not just now, be patient, for there could be new lessons to learn before the help can be given.

We should glide along, in sync with God to keep the peace and harmony in balance. Be careful as he cannot help us if we are filled with anger, rage or resentment. We must accept and believe this is sinful and then hand the negative emotions over to him for healing. Be open and enjoy the wonderful experience of divine guidance. Be mindful of new sounds, visions, feelings, or thoughts.

Believe with confidence; our creator knows we are saints not sinners as long as we travel along the harmonious path, and banish any evil from within.

This day is my first day forward; I will view my past as though it was a movie. As for now, real life is just beginning, will you join me?

Divorce and We Live Again

Is there life after divorce? I did not want the divorce in the first place. I am having trouble letting go. Once I got accustomed to the idea, I thought it would all be perfect. I imagined that as time passed the stress would disappear but the stress is still there, it is just approaching from a different direction.

I am suddenly on my own dealing with issues such as money, bills, and the house maintenance. All totally my responsibility, none of which I have ever experienced before. What if I have to move, maybe even relocate to a different area where house prices are more affordable? I will have to start over again, make new friends. Will I have nice neighbours? What about schools for the children?

I live in fear. I don't think I can cope on my own. Surely my fear will ease with time? If nothing else it has to be better than living in a marriage that was one nightmare after the other.

I have to give myself time. I am starting a new journey; my new pathway will become brighter once I leave the past behind. Close the door and enjoy the journey ahead.

I must not grieve and let any bad feeling fester because the only one who is suffering will be me.

Ban resentment; it must be banished forever otherwise it will devour my whole being.

Even the thought of my 'ex' suffering should not fill me with delight as more negative thoughts will not make me feel any better. Nobody else will be punished for holding on to these feelings, only me.

If I take a negative approach it will only allow for depression to seep in. I must remember I have divorced one person not the entire human race. It is wrong to judge all because of my unfortunate bad experience.

There will always be one bad apple in an orchard of wonderful ripe fruit; the rest are palatable so worth sampling. Just discard them before the core is reached and the rotten fruit appears.

My life isn't finished, it is only that part of my life that is over, the rest of my life begins today and I welcome the good times ahead. I need a period to adjust and treat myself to a positive outlook. The pain will ease and a brighter future awaits.

I know it, I deserve it.

Dreamers

I dream of financial abundance but still it is not falling into place. I cannot believe my talents have not been recognised by anyone apart from my nearest and dearest. Should I give up my quest for stardom? But why would I when I know I am and gifted? I'm certain I am. I deserve to be rich and famous, after all some TV celebrities do not have anywhere near as much talent as I. But wait, is this truly important? Could I really be this shallow? Am I really so arrogant and self-centred? Can I not accept the fact I may just be one of life's average people? Is it so wrong that I find it so difficult to be content with just being middling? Am I just striving to be the best I can, or am I reaching for the unreachable? Should I show myself to the world on one of the TV reality shows? Perhaps this is the answer? Will I find fame this way? Why do I spend so much time dreaming? I feel that life is passing me by. I keep thinking, one day I will be all right. One day I will be the popular one. One day it will all fall into place.

I have an underlying fear that I may become old before I realise I am not as talented as I had once thought. Then to my horror I am too old to start on a new path. Oh why have I wasted so many years?

I must stop being a dreamer. Our creator knows my talents and so I will let him guide me along my destined path; this will bring both peace and harmony and surely that is more important.

(dreamer photo) - by danilo rizzuti

Drug Abuse

Was it the devil's cunning ways that influenced some people to introduce illegal drugs into our lives? Only one so evil would do such a wicked thing; a loving person would not, for their care and concern for others is vital. The devil, on the other hand, desires nothing more than for us to live with pain and suffering, enjoying our misery. If only I had known this. Oh why did it happen to me? If I had more willpower I would have said no.

Surely I am not addicted to drugs. I just need something to make me happy and take away my inner pain. Maybe after my next fix I will give it up. Once more won't hurt; after all I am having such a stressful time and I deserve some freedom from this raging battle in my head.

Sadly, after a while, the gloom has returned with intensity. I know I said I will stop after the last time, but I feel so rotten. Maybe after this one I will feel better and have the strength to stop.

Aaahhh, that's good; I feel happier now.

As time passes it doesn't take long before the sorrow returns. No, oh no, not again. There must be another way?

My friend's say when I have my fix it brings out the intolerable person in me. They say I begin to act really weird and my face turns into what could be described as a distorted ugly troll. Somehow drugs make pretty people ugly, and ugly people even more ugly.

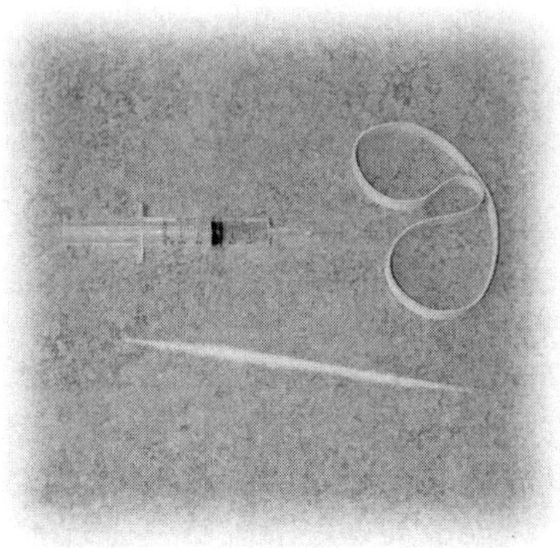

This is not what I planned for myself. As a child I had such wonderful dreams about my future; now it just looks like a very deep black hole. I never wanted to be a slave to anyone or anything, but here I am, a slave to drugs. I do not have control of my life anymore; the drugs have control of me.

Perhaps I should try and untangle why I began to go down this slippery road. Maybe I just wanted to feel better and free of the emotional pain I was in.

I want out but I need help. Will you help me?

Education Life's Tool

I want to broaden my mind, build on my character, fill my brain with information. To do this I know I must focus on my education.

The knowledge needed to gain my qualification could take many years of study and sitting in on numerous lectures and taking numerous exams. Many of us shy away from attending school, why?

The schooling will benefit each and every one of us. So where does the desire come from to skip school when the only one who will suffer is me of course?

I am so lucky. I have the chance and ability to study. I have eyes to see and ears to hear, and with the intervention of the Internet I am now able to explore every corner of the earth for information. It is a marvellous tool, full of data, challenges, experiences and a host of people searching for answers to their questions. So many experts giving advice and passing on their knowledge to others.

My questions are so varied, where do I begin? It is so exciting and yet scary. Am I making the right choices with my selected study subjects? Will they help with the pathway I want to take? Do I know which direction I need to be heading in? As I look ahead to my career path I should be filled with excitement and the motivation to face each day with the eagerness and enthusiasm to make my life purposeful.

I am one of the learners of today and so that potentially makes me one of the leaders of tomorrow.

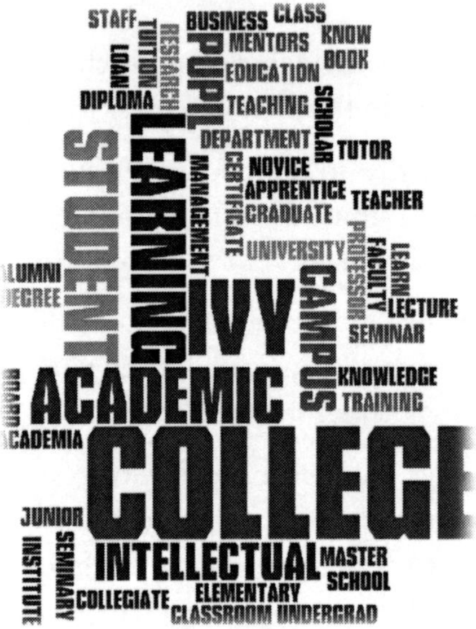

For this reason it is my responsibility to make the most of my education, but still I have allowed another day to drift away as I am still curled up under my duvet as the clock strikes one o'clock.

Tomorrow is approaching fast; I must seize it as it arrives. Today will never come again. When tomorrow has passed it will be left to dwindle away in the ether and become a distant memory for only the history books to recall. Your life is precious so make use of it.

(education photo) - by vectorportal

Ego with a Capital – 'S'

I know my ego will become extremely upset if I live my life filled only with an abundance of love. My ego loathes my harmonious peaceful manner, getting angry if I ever enjoy calm tranquil times, as my ego will no longer flourish.

As my ego regains control, the inflated feeling of superiority towards others begins.

My self-centred behaviour will only gain respect from my ego; others will just avoid me and drift away when they have the chance. Who wants to be around someone who cares little for others? Each one of us has two sides fighting an internal battle; both are struggling to be in the forefront each day.

The passive soul of stillness and wisdom is challenged daily by the screams of rage from our ego. If I listen to the devious false me and let my ego surface, its calculating methods will engulf the quietness of my true inner peaceful self.

Has my ego been playing tricks? I don't feel content. Today I used emotional blackmail to get what I desired. I needed to be noticed and only happy when I was the centre of attention.

I shouldn't, I know, but I do blame others for my unhappy life. Why am I the victim? Poor me; nobody suffers like me.

No wonder I get angry, my life is a mess.

I deserve more, I know I do.

What will make me happy? Am I really this shallow? Could I find contentment in just being 'me'?

The dark negative lure is so strong, how can I resist? The temptation is appealing, to continue being clouded by deep gloom.

In the darkness, there are shadows; to see the shadows there must be light and the tunnel of darkness must hold a light. Keep searching and the light will find you and guide you forward to the warming glow of its shimmering rays.

(ego photo) - by kbayus

Eyes - Gateway to the Soul

Some say our eyes are the gateway to our soul. Is this why we make a judgement just by looking into someone's eyes?

No need for a spoken word, we make an instant judgement if the person is friend or foe.

I'm told certain people have hypnotic eyes. Is this why they are able to influence many to their way of thinking, even though it could be wrong?

The evil eye, in some cultures, is believed to bestow a curse on its victims, bringing bad luck, disease, or even death. Hopefully this is just a myth. What if we are reborn and start a new life on earth? If this is so, perhaps the one thing we keep are our eyes; the windows to the soul. This I guess means people we meet may not recognise the person standing in front of them but as soon as our eyes meet, there is a feeling of familiarity. The memory banks are searched, a distant knowing, that we have met before. When was this meeting? It could have been a very long time ago, perhaps in a previous earthly life.

Does this answer the question why some people I meet make me feel an uneasiness, sometimes even an instant dislike, for no reason that is obvious?

Then there are some people I feel immediately comfortable with, as though I have known them for years.

Our eyes can give the receiver so much information. They show if we are happy or sad, fearful or angry, maybe guilt ridden.

Some people say words that I understand while their eyes are saying something completely different. Do I trust the spoken words or the unspoken words?

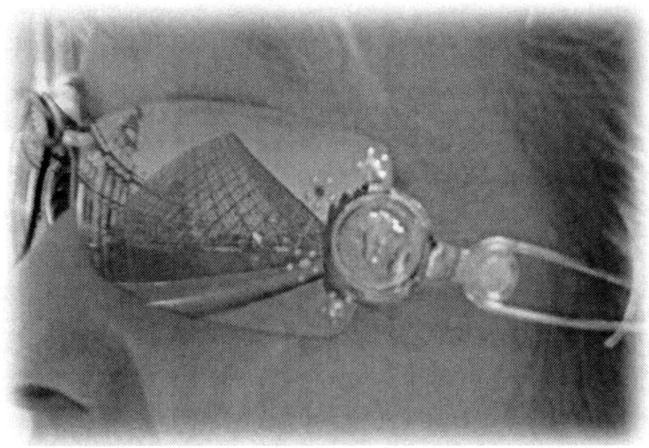

Happiness and laughter can be seen in someone's eyes without having to witness a smile. Let the gateway to your soul shine and bring pleasure to others. Remember, the kindness in your eyes, can be all the comforting words necessary to a friend in need.

Faith Hope and Happiness

What is faith? Is it having sincere belief? Can I trust my faith knowing I have no proof? But wait, I know when I ask for guidance and clarity to see the path to follow; our divine creator is there for me.

My thoughts and ideas are divinely guided but from which direction are they coming? I must listen clearly to my inner voice and not be fooled. If in doubt dismiss it; I know I should.

I must be on guard when I ask for spiritual advice to help me decide which direction my life should take, as the devil can sometimes be waiting in the wings, ready to jump in when the opportunity arises.

My new journey can be nerve-racking, and so I may feel vulnerable. This is when the devil can strike so I must be ready. I must be strong and have faith; my creator with his mighty power will save me from harm. He is pure and full of wonderment. He will protect me when I call upon him. I must be sure to surround myself with a beautiful, solid, full body of armour, and so be protected from the evil forces that can be lurking in the dark damp corners, ready to pounce and drag me down when the opportunity arises.

My faith is the acceptance of the divine power. I trust in my faith to lead me forward along the true path.

I am here to learn, treasure every moment, and fill my life with activities that will help me to grow.

I have the key to beauty and harmony if I just trust in the divine power. The door will be opened; just knock and I will be welcomed in.

My faith will guide me closer to reach my ultimate destiny to find the peace and harmony I need.

faith photo by - courtney rhodes pumpkincat210

Family Tree of Life

They can make us laugh, they can make us cry; they sometimes make us sad, and can often make us mad. But where would we be without them? What is the bond that keeps us together? Some of us rebel and leave our family behind; relocate and move on to a new life.

Why was I born into this family? We are all so different. I wish I were able to mould my family the way I feel they should act, speak, and behave. I try to manipulate them to change but why are they not responding? They seem to be finding this so difficult, can they not see the need to change? Surely it cannot be me that should alter my ways. It must be others that are wrong and need to adjust in order for us to live in harmony; or is it?

Perhaps it is me who is not prepared to listen. Am I even prepared to admit I'm wrong? This is a tough question. Am I strong enough, or wise enough? I think I should take the first step along what appears to be an uneven, rocky path. It won't be easy, but it has to be worthwhile in the long run.

Ultimately the love we share in our families is precious. I should keep reminding myself of this for we are all different and however much we try we cannot control the way other people choose to live their lives.

It is natural to try and hang on to our roots as tightly as we can. As a tree sways in the wind, eventually losing some of its leaves, some to be carried away by the passing breeze never able to return. Others becoming loose, curl up and fall to the ground.

We should embrace our differences, for this completes our life's jigsaw and joins us together as one in the world. We could not progress without all the valuable and varied personality types as there would always be something missing. A jigsaw is not complete without all its pieces.

Once I recognise and accept this my quest for harmony will be easier. I will not be striving for perfection for this can never be.

(family tree of life photo) - by vlado

Father's Bliss

I knew fatherhood would be challenging and that I would make mistakes, but I never knew just how accurate I would be. I have made numerous mistakes, so many I cannot possibly mention them all. I feel despondent; perhaps you can take solace in my regrets?

If I am to learn from my mistakes I should take a moment to weigh up if my next move is the right one. Will my actions have negative or positive consequences? Could there be long-term harmony or damage?

My prime responsibility is to keep my children safe. As they grow I must realise my function is to be their guide. I cannot live their life, that is for them to do; they have been given free will and that is how it should be. They must make their own mistakes which I'm sure will be challenging at times, but they will learn from these mistakes and grow.

It can be a harsh world but I must slacken the rope that binds us together and give them the chance to build their own lives in their own way and not the way I expect them to live.

I know my own father placed my mother at the centre of the home to raise the children, but times have changed. No longer can the father be the only wage earner. To be able to afford the luxury items we all desire, both partners have to work.

Our ancestors may have spoken about the duty of the alpha male and the role of the female, but I am living in the 21st century in the western world.

I have to accept our changing society and adapt accordingly, otherwise I will be constantly climbing a slippery slope and never find contentment.

Fear Consumes my Days

My days are filled with trepidation; it consumes my whole existence. I live in pool of relentless terror where everything I do, everything I say, everything I hear, concerns me. Could this be my fundamental survival mechanism? I wish I could escape from these intense feelings. My only solace is I know I cannot be fearful of my past. My memories are set in my life history, agreeing to own it, then accept it. This is my story and it cannot be changed. I do have some regrets and wish I had been more composed at certain times. The outcome will remain the same despite how often I turn it over and over in my mind; the curtains have been lowered, and the finale has arrived. I cannot fear my past; nevertheless it may sadden me and bring about further despair if I dwell on those gloomy times. My fear can only relate to future events. It may be linked to a present or past action, but it is the future that governs my fear.

Surely if I am worrying about a future event it is driven from my own turbulent thoughts as the event hasn't happened yet. Even if I have a fear of death, perhaps even paint a vivid picture of someone pointing a gun to my head, the fear I have is about a future event. Will they pull the trigger or not? When this panic develops my body becomes rigid like a statue my instinct is to run but I cannot move; my legs turn to jelly and seem like they do not belong to me. My heart is racing, surely soon it will surrender to this rapid beat. I may collapse as every part of my body is shaking.

My breathing is rapid, I am almost hyperventilating and my mouth is dry. I could not cry out even if I wanted to. I need some calm, a guarantee my life is just a piece in a large jigsaw puzzle. Perhaps if I had the assurance there is an afterlife it would make my fears and daily worries seem inconsequential. If I could be certain of my beliefs and trust I am being looked after by a greater power I'm sure I would become less anxious and fearful.

My fears are common to many. I am terrified of snakes and spiders; enclosed spaces send shivers down my spine. I cannot seem to escape from the controller of my fears. Wherever I go, whatever I do, there is nowhere to run, nowhere to hide, as my biggest fear is me.

First Impressions

People often describe themselves by the quantity and value of their possessions; they constantly talk of money, money, money.

I loathe having to listen to their self-absorbed dialogue. They talk of their wealth and status in the community, insist on bragging about how accomplished their family are. We hear of things such as the new sports car they have just purchased, or how many bedrooms their second home has. How shallow it is for someone to think other people are in the slightest bit interested in their materialistic, flamboyant lifestyle.

What I really need is to get to know the real person inside; you were given a beautiful soul so don't waste it.

When I meet someone for the first time I find it awkward trying to make 'small talk'. I am nervous and cautious. Will I like this person; are they someone I could relax with; what type of individual are they; do they have a sense of humour; are they kind to their fellow humans and animals; will they like me?

Shall I approach the meeting with a witty jovial manner, to relax the atmosphere and uncover the genuine inner person?

Could the person standing in front of me have a very quiet nature? Perhaps they are feeling unwell or have worries that are distracting them; this could affect their manner. Maybe someone's loud confident manner is a disguise for an extremely bashful wallflower? This could give a false impression of who they really are.

It is said that you never have a second chance to make a good first impression. If the first meeting is an important one, perhaps a new potential boss, or even a future soul mate, you may never overcome the first hurdle if you miss the opportunity to make a good first impression. What if I blush and mumble my words? Surely this isn't going to create a good first impression.

I cannot be perfect all the time and so I must laugh at my mistakes.

My imperfections are perfect to me, so I must accept them, as I have an abundance of other amazing qualities that outweigh my flaws.

First Love for Me

When I met my first love it happened like a dream. I felt like I was glowing from within; it would make me giggle out loud when I was alone. I knew this love would never end, I had found my heart's desire, and it was my destiny to be with this person.

Before I knew it I had already started practicing using their surname and imagined the wonderful feeling of saying 'I do' at the altar. I pictured how our children would look and what names we would choose. Our house would be a thatched cottage in the country with a white picket fence, a dog and a cat to turn our house into a home. Oh how happily I pictured this scene; who could want for more? Then as time moved on I began to realise this fabulous scene was my dream, and my dream alone. I was speechless when he announced how he had no plans to settle down for many years to come, it felt like my whole life had fallen apart.

That night, I shut myself in my bedroom and cried until I could cry no more. My dreams were shattered; the love of my live had just ruined everything. The person who I thought would be my future partner didn't feel the same, how could I have been so blind. As I lay on my bed I buried my head in the pillow and sobbed until my eyes became puffy and red. My mother entered the room. She knew instantly why I was so upset and she lovingly tried to comfort me saying, 'don't worry my darling, one day you will find your prince'.

So for now I will take a deep breath, dry my tears, as tomorrow is my last day at kindergarten. Next term I begin junior school, so I only have a few more daylight hours to see my first love.

I will be brave and pretend I am not broken-hearted. When the day is through I will have time to attend to my wounded heart. I will never forget my first love, but perhaps I need to grow a little before making any more plans.

Friends and Acquaintances

How long does it take before an acquaintance I know becomes a friend? Have they shown me respect? Are they judgemental? Do they boost my ego or drown me in criticism?

A true friend will enrich my life, not dampen it. They can help to mould me and enhance my good qualities, not smother me and belittle my every action. They will never feel threatened by my success or beauty, but happy that I have been blessed with such wonderful qualities.

Some friends give a little bit more, in anticipation of a return on their investment. This could develop into a feeling of resentment when their good deeds are not appreciated or rewarded. They could harbour these irrational thoughts which can turn into bitterness.

Then there are my acquaintances; those people I like, and often admire, but don't have a strong connection with. I may see someone every day but that doesn't make him or her a friend.

While an acquaintance may talk superficially to me, a genuine friend would be able to share a true and more deep and meaningful conversation.

Real friendship takes time to mature, for the trust to develop so that we will be able to rely on each other in times of need, with unconditional love.

My acquaintances may expect favours and give nothing in return. But I shouldn't generalise, as some acquaintances can turn into wonderful friends once the loyalty has developed.

I know there have been people in the past that have sucked the life force out of me; they have bled me dry and left me feeling like a washed-out rag doll. So now I know to surround myself with friends who are happy within, content with their life, and who view each day as a wonderful new experience. These people are a joy to be around.

(friends & acquaintances photo) - by scott keartavee

Gardeners Delight

As the world emerges from the darkness, and the sun rises, daylight begins to permeate through the glistening dew covered trees. I slowly drink in the wonderful beauty of nature. This daily routine rejuvenates every part of my body; it is Mother Nature at her best.

If, at the very least, I respect nature, I know I will be rewarded, for I will never be poor. No words can begin to describe the wealth I will receive in return; it is unquestionably priceless.

I admire, longingly, a delicate orchid I have before me. This natural free ingenious gift blends a delicate shade of yellow which is then, attractively, infused with a magnificent burst of bright pink as the colour skilfully becomes more random before it merges back in with the yellow. An artist could not have painted a more perfect picture.

How sad I often feel that there are many that choose not to see the magnificence of nature; it is the ultimate in perfection, but neglected by so many.

Now is the time to find yourself a special place, a place sacred to you. It should be full of peace, tranquillity and stillness; not a breath of wind should disturb your special moment for this time - surrounded by nature - belongs to you.

Slowly take in a deep breath, soaking in the beauty around. Hear the distant sound of leaves rustling in the trees, the happy chirping of a nearby bird calling to its mate.

Relax and be at one with the earth around you; gently run your fingers over the top of the moist grass wiping away the dew.

Kick off your shoes and take a walk barefoot in the grass, letting the natural beauty melt away any tensions; savour every minute. Feel blessed to have this time, it is your special place and this moment belongs to you, so enjoy.

Grey People of the World

Am I one of the 'greys' of this world? As a child I believed normal people were dull grey individuals. I would always scurry away from the suggestion of being an average person. The grey folk would get married; have 2.5 children, a dog and a house with a white picket fence. Now as each year drifts into the next, for me, the idea of becoming a 'grey' isn't so scary.

As I get older it seems that time speeds up and I realise I should treasure every new day. The majority of people I meet are 'greys'. These are the average people in their community those who blend into the background; they are not a recluse nor do they have an overbearing, outrageous personality. Being in the limelight can be wearing; celebrities have paparazzi hounding their every move. Likewise, the eccentrics of this world get sneered at for being one of life's misfits, or bullied and laughed at for looking different. I guess this is why the majority of people want to be in the 'grey' camp and stay invisible to the cynical radar.

Do I need to change or is it others that should address their unfair judgmental manner? Perhaps they are the ones who should modify their behaviour. Their damaging comments are surely a reflection of their own inadequacies.

Still, the cycle continues; there will always be new members willing to join the club and that continue to insult their fellow human beings. Every turn of the dial will result in another harmful comment and so sadness will prevail.

From now on I will try and blend in to become a 'Mrs Grey' and so avoid attracting the unhealthy attention from the 'cynical radar club.' How difficult can it be to just have calm in one's life?

I will fight on and search for freedom from discord and never give up hope that I will one day succeed and be happy.

(grey people photo) - by master isolate images

Growing Old

We are destined to grow old; it is the natural order of living and it will happen without us making any effort. It cannot be halted and cannot be beaten; just relax and accept that this is the cycle of life. Treasure the wonderment that growing old brings and cherish the amazing assortment of memories from years gone by. Some may be happy, some may not be, but still, these are the resources that have made you the person you are today. These memories are the building blocks to enhance our souls; to give us greater understanding and knowledge. As the years pass by, we spend more time standing in front of the mirror, smothering on expensive anti-wrinkle creams and layers of makeup, but still the years show through. Underneath the crinkles, the young person still remains; live each day with an open heart and mind, otherwise you are denying yourself an enjoyable future.

If you were born beautiful, this is one of our divine creator's gifts. If your body stays attractive, then be proud you have nurtured this masterpiece and let your efforts shine through.

Difficult situations may arise but do not let them hold you back, not even the arduous events or memories. The past is history, it cannot be changed. However the future is a mystery, so be joyful, you have control of forthcoming memories.

By changing your perception, you can have a dramatic positive influence on your future. You have the power within to remain bright.

View growing old with a sense of humour and feel excited about the wonderful experiences and people you are going to meet. Youthful looks may be a thing of the past, but the beauty within remains.

Next time you see your reflection, just smile and rejoice, and let your inner glory shine through.

Happiness Leads to Contentment

The key to understanding happiness is easy, but sometimes it can be difficult to apply. If I make others happy I receive happiness.

A smile will always be found, just open my heart and there it will be. Sometimes I may need to dig a little deeper, push aside the woes. It will be there if I search hard enough.

Who really cares if I am sad and miserable? My mood may be justified, I may be weighed down with much heartache and the burdens I carry may be full of sorrow and despair. Who cares but I? These are my struggles and mine alone, as it is my inner soul that is hurting.

How sad I would feel if others gained their happiness when I am gone. Am I such a bad person to be around? If I could see myself from afar would I think the same?

It is important to cherish every sunlit hour and aim to fill each moment with a happy memory. Only my heavenly father knows when it is my time to leave this world so I must not depart this life with regrets. Happiness and sorrow walk along parallel paths; side-by-side they travel, when one fades away and falls behind, the other is there ready to take their place and direct the way forward.

Sometimes happiness is storming ahead, leaving sorrow behind, way back in the distance. Then, without realising, sorrow has caught up. I try to sprint away but I am being dragged down.

My feet are heavy, I am being sucked under. I don't want to drown in a pool of sadness, I must let happiness take the lead.

To feel true contentment, I must concentrate on someone other than myself. Cherish these moments, helping others is a joy; bless this time and watch their saddened face turn to utter delight and gratitude. Seeing the results is so rewarding.

Once happiness is attained it needs nurturing, it will not remain without care and attention. Which world do you want to live in, the joyful one, or the gloomy unhappy one? It is for you to choose.

Hatred can Permeate your Soul

Hatred is such a powerful force. It will destroy every ounce of your gentleness if you let it. Will you end up with a sad clown's expression, as the corners of your mouth begin to permanently turn downwards?

Day after day, you carry this heavy weight on your shoulders; as a new day dawns, it feels like another kilo has been added to the sack of bitterness and hatred within.

How do we free ourselves from this turmoil? We only hate those who have played with our emotions. These people have entered and upset our innermost thoughts, and without realising it, we have allowed them to contaminate our heart.

Living with hate in your heart can only cause you pain, you are the only one suffering, nobody else, so why let it permeate your soul. To hold on to this negative emotion allows the perpetrator to have control over your life, is this what you want? They may have mistreated you in the past, but you are continuing to hurt yourself by reliving this experience over and over in your mind. They can never feel your pain; in fact do they even regret their actions for causing these emotions to become such a dominant part of your life?

Heal the inner you, gradually learn to smile again, forgive this person who has caused your pain. This may be challenging, but it is truly for your benefit, otherwise the bitterness will turn you rotten and bitter through and through.

Do not allow the person who caused your pain to enter your life again; they will only fuel your smouldering fire and dampen down your happiness. Just picture them as the foulest foodstuff you can imagine; like a jellied eel with legs. That will bring a smile to your face as your vision of them is so disgusting and degrading you cannot help but giggle at this ridiculous image.

As a gust of wind passes, close your eyes and pray for any negative emotions to leave your body. Let it lift your spirits, and watch any anger drift away; replace it with the peace and harmony you deserve. May love and light enter your life and fill you with serenity.

(hatred photo) - by art makes me smile

Heartache for a Little While Yet

I'm drowning in a thousand fragments of glass; they pierce every part of my body. I am broken, alone, surrounded by unwanted thoughts. I amble along the busy city streets, only managing to stumble my way through the crowds. Everyone is preoccupied in their own world, their own thoughts, having no time for anyone else.

I feel so claustrophobic as I am surrounded by these bustling people, and still I feel so lonely.

I am in one of the world's major cities and yet here I am so very, very alone. My throat feels dry, my tummy aches, my mind is in turmoil. I am tired but I cannot sleep. I try to look to the future, but the past keeps catching up and haunting me.

Please somebody, help me; anybody?

I lay with another but their presence is so cold. How can someone be so near and yet true togetherness seem so far away.

Do they know of my inner suffering? Will the ripping of my heart ever cease? Will I be able to allow the healing to begin, or is my pain so deep no compass will ever be strong enough to locate the source of the grief?

Today I cannot see tomorrow; yesterday is so prominent; how can I find peace from the heartache of yesterday.

Is it the right time for me to be healed or does my heart need to bleed some more?

When it is the right time for me, then I will take action and strive to move forward. I will enlist the help of my dormant unconscious mind to bring warmth back into my life. Slowly, but surely, I will regain the strength to view yesterday as one of my life's lessons.

(heartache photo) - by lau_lau chan

Hero - A Knight to Remember

My hero, my saviour, he leads me gently along the pathway paved with kindness and compassion; I always admire his actions, always selfless, only thinking of others and not himself.

My hero guides others to think clearly, which diverts their concerns, and so they forget about wallowing in their own self-pity. My hero escorts the nation and leads them out of turmoil, but is my hero a hero in my eyes alone?

Others may have a hero they admire; it could be achievements they applaud, charismatic good looks, or willpower and leadership.

My hero is a hero to me, but how do others view my hero? What if my hero is a political or religious activist? They are heroes to their followers whilst to others they could commit evil acts and be classed as terrorists.

My hero has made such a difference in my world; his courage, his continuous fight for justice and peace, what an amazing person, a true inspiration and a leader to follow. His manner is motivating to all who enter his life, never raising his voice or using harsh words always gentle by nature, compassionate, and tenderness is never far away.

You are truly my hero. I am your faithful follower, your loyal companion, and always your devoted friend.

Please will you remain my hero forever, never let me down, and never slip from the pedestal I have put you on?

(hero photo) - by creative tools

History Moulds Our Future

When yesterday and tomorrow are always in the present, does this prevent me from concentrating on the here and now?

I constantly worry about what the future has in store and spend an unnecessary amount of time mourning unhappy previous experiences. I dwell on the sadness and hardship from the passing of time, and so overlook the fact I should be living each new day with enthusiasm and excitement. History is an important part of my present; without my history, how would I have learnt so many important lessons?

Drawing upon, not only my own life's resources gained over the years, but also the experiences of others. I may even be able to avoid making the same mistakes they did.

History will be with me each day that follows; each moment that passes is remembered, some more significant than others, but all count towards my history.

I occasionally make foolish judgements that affect the way I think and behave. I should, instead, embrace this knowledge and so become wiser each and every day that passes. Occasionally, my learning can be tainted, dwelling on the darkness and burying myself in deep gloom and sadness.

The internal battle commences, for I struggle, as I need to drag myself up from the depth of despair, feeling despondent and forlorn.

As history passes, my memory fades; I may still have some hurt to deal with, but hopefully it won't be as painful as time passes.

Bring forward those happy thoughts; embrace and enjoy the wonderful memories; discard the sadness and celebrate the joy the rest of my life will bring.

Home is My Castle

My house is my home, my castle. I may be a temporary occupant in this dwelling but still, it is mine for today, a place I can lock out the rest of the world and delight in the peace and serenity. It may not be a fancy abode, filled with lavish priceless furnishings and antiques. It may be lacking high tech gadgets, but it is still my shining castle. Every device, every piece of furniture, is an extension of me; lovingly cared for until it beams with delight. My possessions have my imprint; the mark I leave has its own identity, its own character, and its own personality and will remain for eternity. My possessions may have many owners in the future, but they will hold my unique, distinctive, individual mark. Will future generations care for my possessions, respect their heritage and lovingly maintain them as if they were new? For they will be the custodians and, soon, my possessions will hold their imprint as the cycle begins once again.

Today, I lovingly hold onto my possessions. When my grasp slowly begins to falter you are welcome to take over. The journey continues.

Hormonal Changing Games

Unsettling times can often be found in our hormonal world within. If challenged, the raging hormones can begin to engulf our entire being. We become engrossed in matters that would normally pass us by, not letting rational thoughts enter our minds, only the illogical ones are allowed to surface.

Warning signs appear, sometimes toxic anger emerges. This unhealthy feeling creeps up from nowhere, getting worse as the minutes pass. The inner battle begins once the fire has been ignited. It feels like my head could explode under the pressure and I wonder if I still have control of my mind. Will my fight or flight instinct triumph? Am I ready to steam ahead or run as far away as I can?

For many years I had been plagued by my monthly cycle. Then, when the ability to bear a child diminishes, new hormonal problems begin; once again I am in complete turmoil.

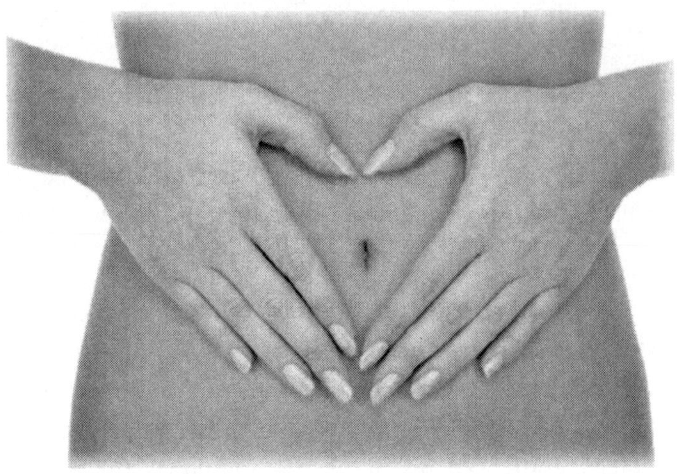

A period of calm arrives, comfort has returned, peace and contentment follows; for how long nobody knows. Enjoy this peaceful time while it lasts.

(hormonal photo) - by ambro

Inner Beauty

Why am I burdened with unhappy thoughts about my appearance? These agonizing whirling feelings cannot change the way I look. My anxiety generates sadness and discontent; does anyone else really care if I am not perfect? I think not. I am the only person who devotes so much wasted time and energy worrying.

I have been blessed with so many wonderful gifts; I should be thankful. If I ignore my flaws and defects it will certainly lead to inner peace and contentment. Others may judge me on the few extra pounds I carry, and the inevitable ageing wrinkled face that comes to us all? If you are someone who is shallow and only concerned with my outer shell, then who needs a friend like you?

Some may not have received the gift of good health; some sadly have been dealt a life with disfigurements, having to suffer ridicule from others just because they don't look perfect.

The beauty we have inside is precious, and that is surely more important. The kindness someone is willing to share and the compassionate smile that emanates from within; their helpfulness and compassion all come from a beautiful, brightness enriched inner soul.

Outer beauty does eventually fade with time; it matters not how much money is spent at the beauty salon, a birth certificate never lies.

Relying on your outer beauty to progress in life could be chancy as your catwalk allure may buckle and be revoked without you even noticing.

I want to reverse the ticking body clock, or, at the very least, slow it down.

My youth is moving further and further away, the wrinkles are increasing, the crevasses becoming deeper and deeper. Oh no don't let it be me; why is my face becoming so drawn and haggard.

Give this ageing process to someone else, spare me this heartache; you are not wanted, not desired, not needed. Thankfully one thing you cannot take away for me is my inner beauty. It is mine, and mine alone. You have no control over it, for it is for me to nurture, cherish and exude to others, to brighten their day, and, for me, I can smile contentedly knowing I have made a difference.

Just for today.

(inner beauty photo) - by koratmember

Inside-Out Pain

How do I control my inner pain? The suppressed, raging, angry bull fighting beneath the surface. Even if I learn to control my anger, I will still experience the full extent of my inner emotions.

The volcano erupts with unhealthy consequences as I find myself saying things I always regret later. I know my boiling button is easily pressed, I just wish it was not so often. How do I find the strength to disarm and defuse the button and so begin to recover? Perhaps I could imagine being someone else, a real person or a character in a play that has the ability to put things right with ease. If I continue to try and race ahead, with emotional baggage weighing me down, it will take a lifetime to work through it.

I need to abandon the baggage before I can move forward. I want that wonderful feeling of contentment to return; I want to feel energized, with vitality coming back into my life, filling my body with happiness and glee.

As this feeling begins to return, I perceive pleasure more often than pain, and solutions rather than complications.

I am making the choice to be happy as bitterness and anger does not resolve the situation; it just fuels the smouldering fire within. The draining merry-go-round of turbulent chaotic thoughts slow and gradually disappear.

My inner pain has eased; it is not good nor bad, it just 'is'. My inner beauty can begin to surface and proudly reveal itself to the outer world.

(inside-out pain photo) - by adamr

Inspiration - or Is It?

Do you follow a faith, or do you believe in a greater power but refuse to give it a label? Perhaps we should call this your 'Homemade DIY faith.'

Do you listen to the quiet voice of your intuition, the gut feelings that appear and cannot be shaken off until actions are taken to address the problem?

Listen to the soft voice of peace and calm, not the bellowing voices of fear.

Some may say the voice of your heart is guiding you, but your head is saying something different. Which one do you follow?

Can you hear those faint whispers, the guidance coming from a higher power, from a being with wisdom beyond belief?

Surely this cannot be? Those clever thoughts, the incredible abundance of knowledge must be coming from me. Am I really that smart or am I being guided by a greater authority?

How often have you cried out in times of need, waiting for the answer you so desperately seek? Who are you looking for, who are you calling out to if you are not the person that holds all the answers? Who are you relying on, who do you turn to in times of need? Perhaps your prayers are not answered because this is the wrong path for you to follow. However hard you may struggle, you are being held back, dragged down, as though you are walking in quicksand.

Perhaps your homemade faith is actually influenced by a greater power, one so much wiser than you or I? Listen to the quiet voices within; the one that gives you true guidance, for this is your perfect inspiration.

(inspiration photo) - by orin zebest

Intimacy is a One-way Ticket

I know once I became intimate, there was no turning back. Nothing more to discover, you have seen it all, every hair on my body, every pimple exposed. This is me, an open book, shaded from all, except you. Now that I am uncovered, will you still desire me, for there is nothing left to be discovered? Will you become uninterested as there are no more challenges, no more intrigues, no more mysteries? I am fearful you will become bored, you have tested the goods and now the passion has been satisfied you will cast me aside, move on to pastures new and so begin the process again.

Oh why oh why did I let my veil slip so easily. I thought this would be applauded, not discarded like a worn out kitchen rag.

I wait by the phone hoping to hear the familiar ring tone assigned to your name so I know without looking it is you who is calling.

The silence is deafening. Not a murmur, not a sound. I will not leave the phone for fear I will miss your call. Still, the silence continues. I cannot bear the shame I feel, the inner anguish, the torment. I bury my head in my pillow hoping this feeling will diminish, but the heartache continues.

I recap the previous night, the build-up to fulfil my raging desire. A gentle smile appears, a warm tender feeling softly engulfs my body, was it really a mistake to allow this night of passion to happen?

I am startled as I hear the phone ring, that familiar tone, could it really be you?

I answer with caution; to my surprise you sound cheerful, I can almost hear the smile that must be beaming across your face.

I then hear the most wonderful words I could possibly wish for.

"Can I see you again?"

Luck has dealt me a card this time and I am eternally grateful.

(intimacy photo) - by gilberto filho

Judgement Day

Should I be concerned that one day my actions will be punished? When will this be, and who will be my judge? Will it be my family or friends? Ought this be where my fear lies, or is there a greater power that I need to be concerned with?
Can I really escape from this inevitable conclusion just waiting to pounce?

Shall I continue along my selfish rocky path, full of deceit and lies, just because so far I have been able to shield myself from being noticed? Am I really so blind to think that my luck will continue?

I am starting to feel uneasy; I know there is a price to pay for my actions, at this moment in time, I just choose to ignore it.

As time passes, I consider my options; perhaps before I have to face my creator I should alter my deceitful ways.

Our heavenly father will pass the verdict, do I really want to wait and see what fate has in store for me?

Making some changes now may ease the confrontation later. I know there are penalties, I just don't want to face up to them.

Would my life be less complicated if I tried to live each day in a manner which is more considerate to others and their needs? For I know at the moment, every which way I turn, trouble is just a little way ahead of me.

Can I really change? Maybe a little each day won't hurt.

In the bible, it indicates in Mark Chapter-9 Verse-1 that judgement may come before I die. Then my efforts will not be in vain.

Perhaps I should take this bible verse seriously and act now before it is too late.

Will you join me?

(judgement day photo) - by watcharakun

Justice for Me

How can I fight for justice with controlled passion, and not be antagonised by others attempting to unsettle my rights for civil liberty? Protecting myself and standing strong in my beliefs; feeling comfortable to speak openly in public with the knowledge that freedom for all is paramount?

I call for peace and justice, not hatred and revenge.

Behind the apparent tranquil exterior I struggle to control this intensifying anger. My voice may appear calm and measured, but let there be no mistake there is much pain and anguish beneath the dark glasses I wear to conceal my tear filled eyes, full of despair.

Justice can often be found when an offender and a victim are joined together. The offender realises the traumatic effect their actions have had on their victim.

Will this bring closure for the victim or just enhance the pain they are feeling? Can I cope with this pending meeting, able to look the perpetrator in the eye and keep my composure?

Have I the strength and willpower not to crumble and fall apart, allow my emotions to run away?

Strength and determination will prevail to change this vision. A dedicated, strong fighting spirit is necessary; the battle needs to be won on behalf of all our innocents around the world.

Join together, standing side by side. The force of this collective, heroic crowd, will overpower the evil in our society.

Justice will always be served; it may not be obvious today, some crimes go unpunished and are left to fester for many years. Does the offender really want to take a chance in thinking their actions have avoided any punishment?

One guarantee we can rely on is that when the day arrives and darkness fades, a glimmer of light reveals a beckoning, bright, glowing passageway; the unpunished crime will be judged.
Justice will now be served.

(justice photo) - by dl brown

Lies Never Disappear only Fade with Time

My body can be likened to a pincushion. The continuing deceitful behaviour and the never-ending lies; each one creating another pinprick, which pierces deep down until it eventually reaches my inner soul. You try to conceal your lies and sometimes you succeed; but sadly you have sown the seed of doubt so that nagging intuitive feeling increases. You become defensive and try to divert the suspicion and avoid the uncomfortable questions; a sure sign my fears are justified; the liar has struck again. This time it could only be a little white lie, but this is just another one added to the pile that is steadily increasing. It seems to be like an addiction; it is easier to fabricate a story rather than tell the truth; why be honest when a lie will do? It is under your skin, you are a compulsive liar, letting it contaminate every part of God's wonderful creation, allowing the dark-side to slowly take control.

Sadly the dishonesties grow, overpowering all the goodness within; contaminating your soul until your whole body is riddled with shadows. The dimming light slowly fades as each day passes; the scam has gradually occupied every part of your being. If you believe these little white lies are harmless, think again; they just merge with all the others, resulting in a huge mass of deceptions. How can you live with this shame? I guess you even lie to yourself? It isn't really harming anyone; is this your justification?

Sadly you are mistaken. The breaking hearts of those closest is clear; they are running out of forgiveness.

If you believe your illusions will fade with time, think again; for only you will know the consequences of your actions when you are all alone to reflect. All your loved ones will have deserted you; they can no longer live with the darkness. You created it; you live with it, as it is for you and you alone.

You and your maker are the only ones who know the truth about the lies you have told. Confront your inner gremlins now.

If you leave it until your last breath, it will truly be a fate much worse than death itself.

You have been warned.

(lies photo) - by national library of norway

Living or Existing

I walk, I talk, I breathe; am I really filled with life or am I just surviving each day? Some are able to live life to the full; others struggle just to make it to the end of each day. Their eyes reflect their sadness, the inner pain torments each day that unfolds.

Instinctively as a child, my whole purpose was to have fun and live each fantasy moment to the full. As time passed, society conditioned my way of thinking. I become one of the many trailing sheep who follow in the pattern of life. I fell in line, it seemed the easiest way. I dressed, not to be noticed, just to blend in with others. My career path was acceptable to my friends and family; I even started dating the average boy close to home, just to fit in and conform.

At the same time each morning the alarm clock awakens me to begin another average, predictable day. Can I honestly say my time is filled wisely? Experiencing every moment, living life to the full? Or is my routine driving me into a deep, dark, desperate gloom?

Existing is only occupying space and time; undetected my presence has little impact on the world around me. Very little effort is needed to survive but if I made some meaningful changes my life could turn around and begin to shine.

Taking notice of my surrounding world, enjoying the beautiful countryside, appreciating the wonderful heritage we have. These are all the foundations I need. A smile and a kind gesture will give a sparkle of hope to others. There is no reason or motive, just setting in motion the snowball effect, to help extinguish the darkness, allowing the light to shine through.

My first duty is to start investing in me, learning to love myself, becoming contented in my own skin and enjoying my own company. I have the necessary tools for my life to truly begin.

Love Conquers All

The love from your partner can fill many vacuums, but not all; we need many unique forms of love. The love from our parents is different from the special love we have for our children; which in turn is different to the love we receive from friends and even from our pets.

It is impossible and unfair to expect our partners to satisfy all our love chambers. A single person does not have all the necessary tools to fulfil and satisfy all our love compartments.

Your emotional needs are different from those of others; what is missing in your life could be unimportant in someone else's.

Your inner soul knows what love it yearns for; just open your heart to receive the wonderful warm glow that can only be experienced with love.

Often people want to block the channels of love, not wanting to be exposed to potential heartache. Free yourself and loosen the shackles; take a chance with love. It could leave you exposed, but if you do not take the risk how will you ever know if it could be one of the most wonderful times of your life when every second just feels perfect.

Love will triumph; joy and delight will satisfy all. Be careful, and avoid the ever-willing evil one; you may find love, but love from the dark side is full of sadness and heartache.

Deep inside, there is always a quiet voice eager to surface, desperate to overpower the darkness.

Hold onto the inner voice, for this is the real you. Make your love alive; feel the sparks tingling along your spine; run in the wind, laugh out loud, jump for joy, for this is your new beginning, so enjoy.

Loyal Companions

The death of my beloved canine companions was just as heart breaking as when I had to cope with the loss of one of my relatives. Some may find this hard to understand; after all they were 'just dogs' but I feel privileged to have had this joyous relationship. This unconditional love can only be appreciated by someone who has had a similar experience. These wonderful gifts from God were always waiting when I walked through the door each day. The loyalty and love would be there no matter how dishevelled I looked; I would still be greeted with a big smile and a wagging tail. I had a number of warning signs a few days before their parting; I believe it was their way to prepare me they had to go.

After my beautiful companions died, I realised they all cheated death many times. On each occasion I tried to prepare myself, it could be the end; then to my amazement, they would bounce back and this always came as a blessing. Soon they would be back to their normal mischievous selves, demanding food, love and attention.

When the obvious signs appear and it is their time to go, I must try to accept this and understand they have to leave. Their body is weak and can no longer house their wonderfully gentle kind spirit. However much I want them to stay, I must give my approval for them to leave. They must not suffer; instead, if it is necessary, give them the greatest gift of all and agree to have them put to sleep.

They may try to hang on but their body is ready to depart as it is just tired out.

When the inevitable happens and they leave this world, try to remember the happy times. There is no need to feel guilty if you have to make the decision to put them to sleep. They know you are doing this out of kindness so they do not suffer more than they have to.

Never feel uncomfortable about getting another loyal companion, there is enough space in your heart to continue loving your deceased pet and the new one. Give yourself time to grieve, and do not feel embarrassed in front of others if your heart is breaking; believe me, there are many, many people who have gone through the same as you and I. It is natural to feel such extreme sadness. If you are feeling the loss, I share in your grief and surround you with warmth, love, compassion and friendship.

(I dedicate this verse to our wonderful departed companions: Jenson, Bonnie and Darcey, who appear in this photograph with my husband David. You are in our thoughts every day. Let us hold on to the happy memories until we are together once again.)

Materialistic Merry-go-Round

I am still waiting for that special moment to arrive, when my material possessions fill my inner vacuum. I believed buying expensive designer clothes and jewellery would make me feel ecstatic and generate the happiness I so eagerly desired. But could my obsession to buy these materialistic objects actually be increasing my internal suffering? I know I have beautiful possessions, but are they really the key to fulfilling my needs? I feel lost, this emptiness is destroying me; I desperately want to find my inner peace.

I am so discontented; I crave more money so I can buy more possessions, which I mistakenly assume will make me happy. Surely some new purchases will help boost my low self-esteem and increase my confidence. I remember my dear old grandmother would often talk of the financial struggles she had during her early years of marriage. My grandpa would be out working whilst my grandma remained at home to care for the children, but they were content and happy with what they had.

I think conventional housewives like my grandmother are slowly diminishing in numbers, almost obsolete. No replacement parts are available to rebuild and replicate the housewife of this bygone era.

Oh, why do I still feel dissatisfied? My shiny new possessions temporarily fill a void. I wish I knew how else to fill this emptiness to get the same feeling of satisfaction that I have when I return home from shopping with my bags filled with so many goodies. The pleasure lasts a short while; as soon as the purchase show on my credit card statement the satisfaction has gone. Now I feel more depressed as I have spent money I didn't have. Oh please help me stop this never-ending cycle, and find real contentment to ease my inner despair.

(materialistic photo) - by image_of_money

Men'On'pause

Oh what is happening to me?

I seem to become hot and flustered without warning.
Oh what is happening to me?

Now I can't seem to fit into my clothes anymore; the zipper starts to move, then slowly grinds to a halt as it catches on a chunk of blubber that has recently appeared around my middle.

If this wasn't bad enough my husband is always making me mad, he irritates me all the time, why oh why does he do this? I wonder, could it be my tolerance level is below zero.

The thought of making love with my husband used to fill me with delight, being close to him and loving his tender touch. Now to curl up in bed with a good book and a cup of cocoa, is much more appealing.

The get-up-and go I once had, has got up and gone. Not an ounce of motivation is left; will I ever feel human again.

Oh what is happening to me?

My youth has gone, my reflection no longer smiles back at me. Now enters the dreaded 'change' accompanied by a new me who looks like a hunch-backed sweaty old hag, carrying a pitchfork and willing to use it on anyone who happens to cross my path.

Oh what is happening to me?

Can I view the menopause as an opportunity? In my many years I have gained maturity, wisdom, and knowledge. I am blessed with an abundance of friends and hold many happy memories. It's a time to have more freedom and bring joy back into my life. Let's pray my hormones settle down soon and normality returns.

(menopause photo) - by tobyotters photostream

Mirrors Reflect My Inner Self

I can transform my past, not by time-travel, just by changing the way I view my previous experiences. My reflection stays with me wherever I go; I wish I could discard the old mirror, as I no longer wish to see my image looking back at me. This one is full of sadness and holds bitter memories. I want a new reflection that shows a beaming smile when I view my past learning experiences. Is it a crime just to want to alter how I feel about my past?

Some memories bring back sadness, and often stir up anger and hatred towards my wrongdoer. I feel ashamed about some memories, and embarrassed by others because of how I have behaved in the past. All I want to do is bury my head in my hands and hope the memory fades quickly without leaving any residue.

If it hurts this much, then I must change the way I think about my past actions. Accept my behaviour was not gracious, make peace with my inner thoughts, and banish my inner demons. If I take no action the heartache will continue, constantly hounding my every thought and eventually rip my emotions to shreds.

I can rewrite the despair from my past, the fight can still be won: I just need to train my beliefs to be positive, rather than negative, and then I can meditate with a clear vision, synchronize my thoughts with my creator and welcome the guidance offered with gratitude.

Perhaps if I show genuine remorse I may even receive forgiveness and so make a fresh start leaving the pain and anguish behind. Will you have mercy on me? Can you forgive me?

I have been punished enough in my dreams; my subconscious mind has chastised my actions and corrected my unkind thoughts.

I pray for freedom, freedom from within, as my inner demons are far more harmful than any evil person I may encounter in our world today.

(mirror photo) - by gravitat_off

Mosaic of Life

Where there is light you will also find shadows. Our daily lives will be surrounded and remain in the shadows unless you allow the brightness to penetrate through.

Once you release the darkness from your life and let the light flood through, you will begin to love yourself for who you really are; the joy you feel will bring the harmony you desire.

Train and hardwire your brain to have positive thoughts and to seek out the pleasure you need.

Create your life like a full colour movie rather than a black and white image. Bring vibrant colour and happiness to each day, leave any dark and gloomy days in the past where they belong. Keeping them as a reminder will only drag you down, eat away at your inner peace, and destroy all harmony within.

Your soul has to be nourished, nurtured, and cleansed. It is like listening to the sound of a wonderful orchestra; they may hit the same perfect notes as a computer generated piece of music but the computer has no soul; it can never make you feel as though the hairs are standing up on the back of your neck.

No matter how hard we try, if we are heading in the wrong direction, nothing but obstacles will trip us along the way.

You can battle as much as you like, but you will never reach your goal if your soul desires a different plan for you. Listen to your inner voice, as this will guide you on the correct path to reach your purpose and the road will be a lot brighter and less hazardous.

Try and change any negative experiences into positive ones. Two people can experience the same ordeal; it is how they recall and interpret the incident, whether it will affect their future or not.

Alter your view of any past negative event by seeing them as valuable lessons. You have all the tools needed to be in control of your destiny. Be strong and above all, be positive.

Mother's Pride

The sparkle emerges, the brightness so powerful, as the joy of becoming a mother shine through. The value for this total happiness is priceless.

The bond begins from the first moment the baby is placed in the mother's arms; this is the ultimate contentment.

Then life gets in the way of this special bond, and the baby may be placed in the middle of a parental battle. Mother and father can no longer live together but they have the joint responsibility to care for the child.

The stress is intense; as the mother deals with the pain often experienced during these times, she may even be vindictive enough to turn the child against its father, purely because of her own dislike of the man. That does not justify influencing a vulnerable child, how cruel can she be?

How often I see the cord that binds mother and child become tattered, worn-out, and frayed around the edges.

The harmonious strong bond that once shone becomes strained; tension between mother and child is apparent to all and sometimes resentment develops, turning into dislike, even hatred.

The love could still be there but it is clouded and buried so deep underneath the bitterness; it is hard to believe it ever existed.

The guilty feelings grow, as the damaging emotions increase, and resentment sets in. How can the love still be there with such anger in the shadows increasingly becoming the driving force? I want that loving bond to return, and to discard these dreadful, harmful, inner emotions.

I want my mummy back.

(mothers pride photo) - by state library of victoria collections

My World

Past experiences have influenced my life but I am still ultimately responsible for who I become in the future.

I may have to leave people and possessions behind to continue this journey. Sometimes I am at my loneliest when I have lived with someone. Ignoring the signs and continuing down the wrong road will just result in more obstacles thrown into my path to trip me up along the way.

Ultimately I must find the truth, when the clouds clear and the shadows disappear, then it will be my time to take action.

I desire the feeling of confidence and happiness, to sing during a tornado, smile when the thunder roars, and relax when a bolt of lightning strikes. The storm is part of life; we are always living on the edge of the wind of a hurricane.

God is close by but will not interfere, so don't let the storm pull you down, keep your trust in God.

Most people live in one camp or the other: light or darkness; it is difficult to live in the grey area. Light has to be viewed through darkness, for light can only be seen where there are shadows.

The light may expose areas I would prefer to keep hidden but as the shadows fade the light shines through with warmth and intensity once more.

Stay away from the power of the storm, there is always calm after a storm. Be patient, tranquillity will return.

Nature and its Beauty is Priceless

Preserving nature is one of the most important parts of our life. Its breath-taking beauty is immeasurable. It is important to respect and protect our God-given countryside: to keep it safe, now, and for generations to come.

As every dawn breaks, take a long, slow, deep, breath as you stand back and admire its splendour. Notice, as each new day arrives, how nature has transformed itself once again.

As the hands on the clock face turn, there is something fresh to see; new shapes emerge, blossom materializes, the leaves change colour as a new season approaches.

Without realising it, nature has a wonderful influence on our mood; seeing the bright sunshine makes us all smile; a starlight night makes us feel romantic; a wet cloudy day can make us feel gloomy; whilst a storm can make us fearful. Bless our wonderful world in all its glory.

When we hold the title deed to some land we feel proud of ourselves, however the air we breathe, belongs to each and every one of us. Then why are we so determined to destroy this precious commodity? We pump pollutants into the atmosphere and expect nature to accept it and deal with it, but this is not what nature intended.

Air is priceless; we must not poison it with chemicals.

Products from combustion are released, but who really complains when we fill up our vehicle at the nearest petrol station. All we want is to be transported from A to B.

Nature has been here from the beginning of time and will be here until the end. Let it remain as beautiful as it is now, for without your help in preserving its grace, it will crumble and fall, never to be seen again.

Negative Emotions

No, not me, I am not negative. Sure I can be angry at times, or sad; often frustrated and perhaps disappointed when things don't go my way, but negative? Surely not!

I know I am a worrier; in fact I worry every minute of every day, but am I negative? Surely not!

We can all be jealous of others and yes, I am no different from the next person. Does this make me negative? Surely not!

I know I have the power to change, but how? My world seems filled to the brim with misery and hardship; I have no time to relax, no time for me, and no time to change.

My facial expressions can be read so easily, often conveying my anger or sadness. If I had good conversational skills I would be able to express my emotional needs and therefore have a better chance of finding the key to unlocking the safe that hides them so well. This may also open the door to receiving help from others.

Why am I the only one who has so much to do? Nobody else is as busy as me; my life is such a strain. I do not have time to worry about what is happening in the outside world, it is irrelevant. If only I could find love, peace, and harmony from within, it would give me the strength and power to live the life I honestly deserve.

I still feel like a prisoner in my own body. I cannot escape from the rotting feeling of resentment and bitterness. Am I negative; surely not?

Life is not about waiting for the right time to act. If I do have negative emotions then I must find the courage and strength to release them now. If not, I will be powerless in my quest to reach my innermost wants and needs for a tranquil life; the rest of my life begins today.

(negative photo) - by lauralewis23

Nursing the Weak

I decided to invest my energy into helping others to bring me closer to complete excellence.

However, even though the work is rewarding, at times it is frustrating. When I decided to walk this path did I really imagine my vocation would actually include so much time doing paperwork? I should be caring for the sick not stuck behind a computer screen completing form after form after form.

There are few professions that offer such rewards; I have an incredible feeling of satisfaction when caring for others in times of need.

There the patients lie, helpless in their beds, lined up in the ward, just waiting, waiting waiting. Some expecting to see the ward doctor, some nervously anticipating the porter to arrive to transport them to the theatre for surgery, some just waiting for, I know not what.

I arrive home after finishing a long, tiring, ten hour shift and sit and reflect on my day.

As I recall my activities I pop the cork on a bottle of Chardonnay; I fill a tall slender wine glass and take a long, satisfying sip. As I do, an overwhelming sadness emerges.

Without warning my mind returns to the hospital ward, and in particular to the little man in bed four. We all desperately fought to save the poor chap as he had not regained consciousness after taking a turn for the worse the previous night.

After the alarms sounded on the monitor we knew something was wrong.

We desperately tried to resuscitate him, but his body had given up the fight. His heart took its last beat then sadly he drifted away.

I was grateful he passed peacefully, as his wife and children were at his bedside.

To our little man in bed four, my thoughts and prayers are with you and your family. I pray you are now in a place where you are free; free from pain and sadness.

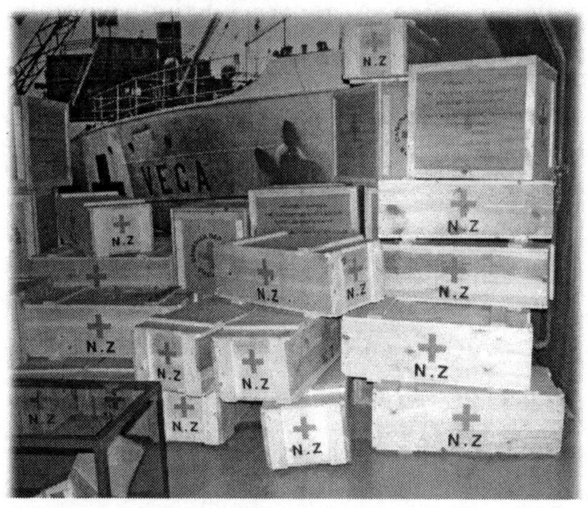

As I take another sip of wine, I begin to forgive myself for the guilt I feel, as I was unable to save the little man in bed four.

No medical advancements can alter the inevitable, no magic, no faith, can change the outcome. Sadly one thing is for sure, we all have to die eventually.

I am grateful I have been given this gift to be able to nurse the living, and to have the compassion and the ability to care for the ones whose days are nearing the end.

(nursing the weak photo) - by naypong

Operation

I sit behind the closed curtain that divides my bed from the one next door. I lie in the standard issue hospital gown, waiting in anticipation, nervous and on edge. The clock is ticking and it will not be long now before it is my turn to be wheeled down the corridor to the operating theatre.

The ward is busy with bustling nurses; I hear footsteps, are they heading my way? I listen as they become louder and louder, the footsteps are accompanied by the familiar sound of the squeaky wheel on the porter's trolley. I take a deep breath and wait, wondering if it is my name that will be called out. The sound of the footsteps begins to fade, growing softer and softer, as they walk past.

I watch the hands of the clock on the wall, how slowly they appear to be moving; the waiting is agonising.

Without realising, I drift off to sleep and fall into the realms of unconscious calm. The anaesthetic the nurse gave me a while ago must be taking effect. For this brief period I am at peace, content in my wonderful dream filled sleep.

That same squeaky wheel on the approaching hospital porter's trolley suddenly awakens me. The squeak begins to slow down until it grinds to a definite halt. The curtain moves slightly as I realise someone is on the other side, then before I can take another breath, a short tubby man appears between the slits of the curtain. He is dressed in green overalls and instantly I feel at ease with this man.

I am greeted with a gentle smile as he introduces himself. He will be leading me along the long corridor towards the operating theatre.

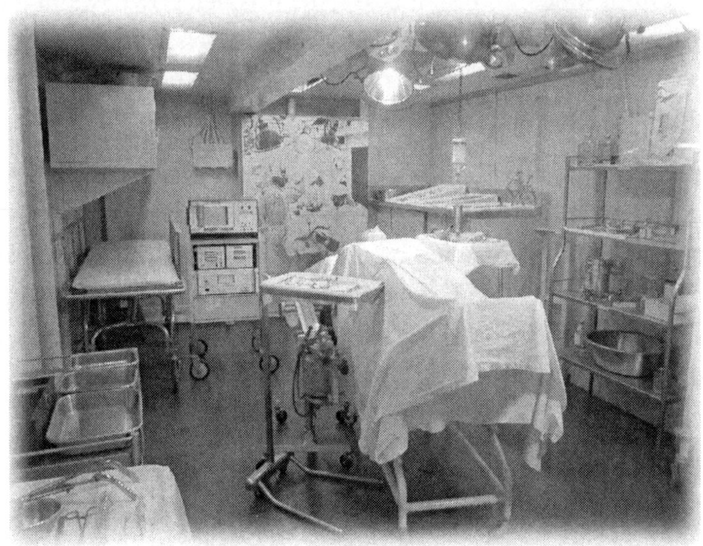

Now I have to put my faith in others as this is out of my control. Am I fearful? Yes of course, but I know that after the operation I will feel so much better. I put my trust in you, as I slip away into the silent world.

Ownership

It is mine and mine alone.

Leave that alone as well; keep out and keep off, my possessions are for me and me alone.

It is not for you to question why I like to keep my possessions all for myself, for if this is my desire then so be it.

They are extensions of me, I have made my mark, left my imprint, and my spiritual residue has soaked into every nook and cranny. If you take them away then you are robbing part of me; how could you be so cruel.

If a thief were to break into my home and rummage through my belongings, then they would be disrespecting not only my home but me also. Every part of my body would be violated, for they have smothered all my possessions with their DNA.

To allow another human being to be this close should be out of choice, not be forced upon by someone else.

If you steal from another it will pollute your soul and destroy every ounce of decency. Break away from the evil forces; start by giving to others not stealing from them. It will cleanse your soul and nourish your heart, and satisfy your mind with pride and fulfilment.

Leave my possessions alone; for while they are of little value to you.
To me they are my world.

(ownership photo) - by jannoon028

Pain - the Never Ending Drumbeat

As my pain grows, I instinctively reach for the source of the drumbeat and press on the area, desperate to relieve the pain. This is nature's way to warn me of the dis-harmony within.

Pain is good; pain is part of my body's defence system. It is there to warn me of a potential threat and is vital for my survival.

How do I describe the discomfort I am feeling? I find it so difficult to put into words. My doctor may say, "What sort of hurt is it?" All I want to say is, "it is a pain that hurts, so get rid of it," but what am I being warned of?

Taking a pain killer will not get rid of the cause; it will just mask the discomfort, so I must pay attention to the warnings, as it may be a signal to take notice, as action may be required.

Nobody can see my agony, so how can they understand the discomfort I am experiencing. One person's pain is theirs, and theirs alone. Nobody feels my pain the way I do. Just because someone else has the same illness or injury, this does not mean my suffering feels the same.

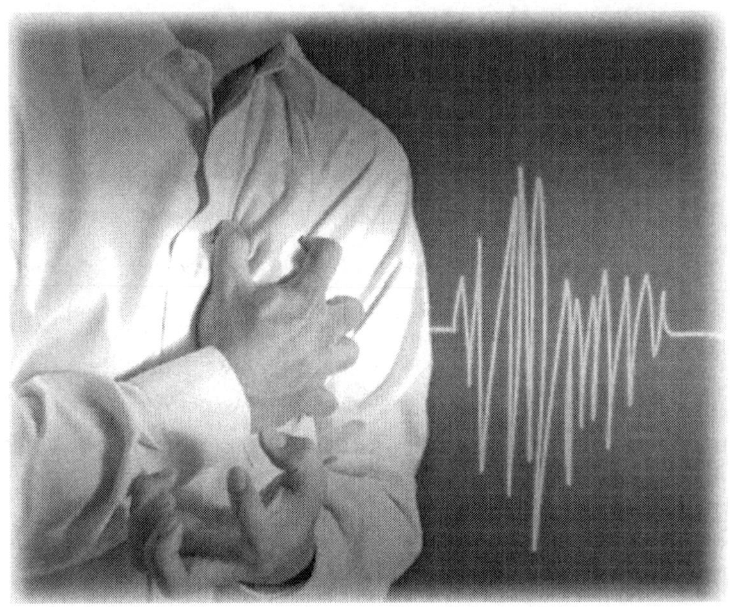

Even though I know it is my body's way of warning me, I cannot thank it, I am never pleased with this discomfort. I can never say to my pain, "Oh thank you for hurting so much, for you are warning me of a problem".

So I just have to live with it when it comes, as more often than not it eventually fades; until the next time.

(pain photo) - by naypong

Passion for Fashion

Fashion fascinates all, not just the critics or the paparazzi who often have a field day criticizing a celebrity's bad dress sense.

All of us appreciate, and admire, a striking outfit, sometimes even feeling envy.

It takes courage and effort to wear something out of the ordinary; being elegant isn't easy, it is an art. This art needs nurturing and time to develop one's style; experiment with colour and texture until perfection is reached.

Some people dress to be noticed, perhaps to seduce their audience. My outfits are an extension of me; they act as status symbols representing who I am.

I want to broadcast to the world. "I am worth every penny I paid for this pair of fabulous designer shoes I'm wearing".

It doesn't matter where you are in the world, fashion is a common language recognised by all. A first impression can be made only once so make the most of it.

Everyone you meet will know something about you just by the clothes you wear. Your lifestyle will shine through and your confident manner will be recognizable to your audience. Your style radiates the message that you are a successful member of your social class.

Find a style that suits you, not what society dictates. Be free, be unique; enjoy just being you.

Peace - will the Dove Return After the End?

Will I be able to breathe deeply, without panic setting in, will I ever smile again, and will I ever feel comfortable and safe again?

Can I believe and trust in the prophecies that tell of major changes taking place to our planet, as the predicted years of change come to a close.

Some say we are heading for major weather changes; tsunamis and earthquakes will shake us all like never before; cyclones with a power and strength beyond our comprehension.

There will be nowhere to hide, no stone will be left unturned. The predictions say little of the nothingness that we may be faced with afterwards.

Perhaps the fear is unfounded; maybe we should welcome the change and start a new life rather than live in fear of the potential devastation.

The change could leave behind, a distant memory; all the hatred, jealousy and countless wars. How wonderful this would be, to live in a safe secure world where there is no more heartache; surely this must be too good to be true?

We can never find complete peace in the outside world, until we have harmony and contentment within ourselves.

Enjoy every moment and be kind to one and all. Do not cause others heartache but follow the teaching of the Ten Commandments and you can't go far wrong. Do you really want to take a chance and wait to see if you will be saved when the change comes?

If you were the commander-in-chief, do you really think you deserve to be saved, or would someone more worthy be higher on the list?

(peace photo) · by harlequeen

Perfect to Me

Who is to say what perfect is; my perfect is perfect for me.

If I don't like my reflection when I look in the mirror and feel it is far from perfect, then why should I think everything I say is perfect? I say it, so I must mean it, so that makes it perfect does it not? Well, for me at least.

Why are we all so desperate to be faultless in all we say and all we do, not accepting our failings? Could it be we are in denial of our own shortcomings?

How do we measure perfection? Who decides what is the ultimate to strive for? Is it just to try and achieve more and more and beat the level of achievements of others? Why is there the need to jump higher, or run faster, or have a bigger house and a faster car than our neighbours; does anyone have an answer?

'Perfect' in my eyes, can change. My first love was perfect in every way until time passed and then the realisation emerged that they were not as perfect as I first thought. Their halo then slips a little so no more are they my perfect person.

Some settle for less than perfect. Is it good to compromise, or should I always strive for perfection? But how can I be content with anything less than perfect. Perhaps I feel my search for perfection may be pointless, as it may never happen. Should I then settle for what I have been dealt, be as happy as I can and just settle for who I am?

If I could create the perfect inner person, then the importance to have materialistic status symbols would become unimportant as ultimately when I leave this life I will leave with nothing. Whatever happens thereafter, and wherever I go, a blank canvas begins again.

(perfect photo) - by photostock

Personality

I am not sure if the enemy I battle inside is real, or is it my personality tempting me towards sin. I feel like an unruly child that has been without good parenting. This child wants, no, demands, material possessions but does not feel satisfied once it has these shiny new objects. In time I just become frustrated and distressed, as my desires need to be filled again.

This constant craving for material goods to give me the happiness I need is not working. I have tried in the same way with my partners. I am searching for the perfect companion who will make me extremely happy forever and ever.

Sadly, I am finding relationships are never like a romantic novel when the woman looks dreamily into the eyes of her hero, desiring to be close, and imagines making love under the stars. However much I am told that good relationships require nurturing and communication, I don't feel I have the patience. If only I didn't have worries I would be happy, but then again I could achieve happiness by dealing with my problems instead of brushing them under the carpet.

My personality isn't naturally good or bad, it's my choice which path I follow.

I have the option to take the easy route or suffer a little. Ultimately I have the gratification that I can live a full and happy life, knowing I am not harming anyone. I am not breaking any laws and, above all, I can sleep at night with a clear conscience; can you?

(personality photo) - by shermeee

Plastic People

Are you obsessed with your appearance, so much so that, you have succumbed to the sharp end of the surgeon's knife?

Oh how I wish society didn't place such pressure on women to look beautiful, and why is it people care less about the appearance of men; it is just not fair.

Even though we all know most photographed celebrities on the covers of glossy magazines are airbrushed, we still want to look as good as they do. We want to be as perfect as they, with a flawless complexion and a gorgeously trim figure. In the movies women look stunning first thing in the morning as they fling back the duvet in a bedroom scene. So why is it I look like a troll that has suffered an almighty fright?

Will I ever be happy with myself? Are we all caught up in an epidemic where there is no end in sight? Will the desire to look perfect ever stop?

I want to blame someone for my dissatisfaction. Do I blame men or what is published in the media? The broadcast pictures of these perfect women on TV making the average girl feel like a fat, ugly blob.

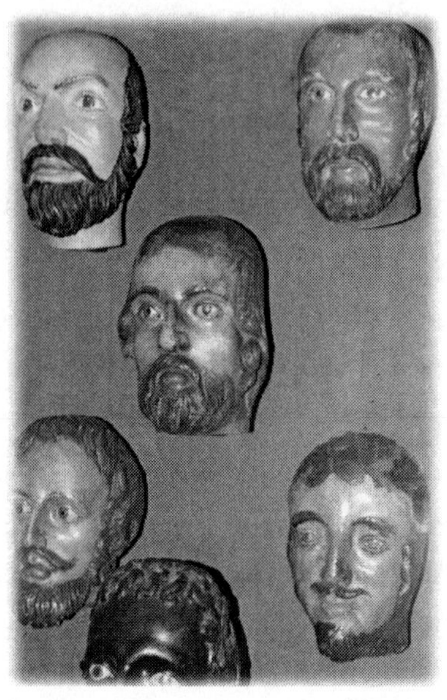

Men make women feel bad about themselves by ogling these beautiful airbrushed females. Is this why so many women are turning to the surgeon's knife to improve the way they look, or spending a fortune on quick fix wrinkle reduction creams?

Let's be honest, would you really put yourself through the horror of surgery if it weren't for the pressures being put upon us? I don't think so! Let us live gracefully with our aging exterior, if you allow our inner beauty to shine through, I guarantee it will make you happy.

Price of Rest

A lazy summer's day invites us to sit and unwind in the wonderful rays of the sun. I sip a long, tall glass of iced lemon tea, the freshness of the lemons tingle my taste buds. I begin to feel all my tension slowly drift away. I look around, as other people pass me by. They look happy, not rushed, but content to stroll along and enjoy the sunshine.

I meet many sparkling eyes, and peaceful expressions; it's a joy to see as this means these people, at this very moment in time, are stress-free and in high spirits.

Sadly, as the day draws to a close, they leave this tranquil setting and return to their normal hectic day-to-day existence; their smiles slowly diminish and their happiness begins to fade.

If only I could capture this wonderful relaxed feeling, I would scatter the sunshine dust into the passing breeze, bringing back joy and happiness to all. Imagine if you were walking through a field full of sunshine dust, the first step you take is filled with joy and the next is harmony, followed by peace and comfort, how wonderful this would be. Take a moment to clear your mind, let the dust settle and be thankful for this harmonious time.

Your stroll can last as long as you like, just cherish and enjoy each slow meaningful step.

When your walk has ended, save a little sunshine dust for another day and share some with others who enter your life. Some may stay for a while; others are just passing through on their own adventure.

Enjoy each moment together and don't be sad when they go, as they are only here for a little while.

Pride in your Country?

Has my opinion altered as time passes by?

Do I honestly still feel proud of my homeland or am I ashamed of my surroundings and the people who live close by?

As I recall the days leading up to a recent royal wedding I felt like I could burst with excitement, as the whole country would be celebrating. On the day of the wedding we were patiently standing behind the crowd control barriers, eagerly awaiting the arrival of the royal party. A gentle nervous tingling began to surface in my tummy, then a lump arose in my throat. I tried to fight back the tears of pride and joy as the procession passed us by; how wonderful they both looked, how proud I feel at this very moment.

As I grow older, my joyful days are becoming fewer and fewer, each day drifting into the next one. My happy nature is becoming a thing of the past. I am just going through the motions of life, not really appreciating my existence, just trudging along as best I can.

As I look around I just do not recognise this country anymore, our culture is being overpowered and suffocated.

Sadly I feel our time has almost passed to restore our peaceful lives; our heritage is being suppressed and may not survive. My country is slowly, but surely, sinking into the depths of despair. The only things left for us to feel proud of are our magnificent historical buildings.

These wonderful treasures have stood for so many years, outliving many people along the way. Will they still be standing for the next generation to admire? Only time will tell. Will my pride ever return; will you care enough to help me?

Without your help, I am just a quiet lonely voice. Help me while we still have a say, for tomorrow we may be totally dumb.

Wherever you lay your head and rest for the night; be proud of your surroundings and have pleasure in what you see. We can all be happy and live harmoniously if we try. Do not let our heritage disappear and be forgotten; act now before it is gone forever.

Protection from the Unknown

Who do I turn to when evil spiritual forces are at play? They can create havoc if we allow them.

Why do I sometimes wake up with an unexplained feeling of foreboding? Have the little devils been playing with my mind whilst I was asleep?

As the day passes, I wonder if the devil is taking a stronger hold on me. Am I his next victim? Vulnerable people, not recognising that evil is taking over, soon become engulfed by its wicked ways. Every part of their mind and body is infected.

I hesitate to watch the daily news as there are more reports on vicious attacks and bloodshed; this is pure evil at play yet again. Are they being influenced by the devil? What other explanation could there be?

The unseen devious fungus of evil can spread through someone's body. As it crawls along every vein, it increases in size and strength. Every organ is contaminated, and every part of the mind and soul. Multiplying as it passes through the body, eventually there is no more light, only darkness.

We must not be tempted by this wicked source of love, we must not be deceived. This love appears alluring but it could be coming from the evil camp.

The devil will show us all love, but it is love for the wrong reasons. The Antichrist pollutes our ego and, if we allow it to surface, he will poison the true you. Banish this impostor; keep the ego buried deep down and locked away; only heartache will come from releasing him.

If we ignore the warnings it can only result in having to suffer the consequences later.

Remember: selflessness diminishes sin and suppresses our ego.

Purpose

Why do I feel like my life is on hold? I glance around and others seem to have lives full of purpose and meaning. I try to figure out why this could be; my mind is in turmoil, I am on a rollercoaster, a whirlwind not wanting to stop. The knots in my tummy are tying themselves into even tighter knots. I realise there is a void in my life that needs to be filled. I ask for guidance, I am desperate, which way do I turn, can anybody help me? I am tumbling further and further into a black hole.

Where do I find the answer? I grasp at the very last straw; I cannot hang on, it is slipping through my fingers, I am sinking down and down, but wait; could there be a glimmer of hope?

I wipe my eyes to clear the moisture; I slowly begin to focus, could it be? I search inside to the depth of my soul. Could there be a flutter, a spark? A smile begins to appear. I feel my heart beat faster. I can see a speck of light in the tunnel, slowly becoming brighter; it is glowing, I can feel its warmth.

My faith and trust increases, there is hope, my confidence is beginning to shine, my head is lifted higher than I ever felt possible. I have found the first step, I have found my faith.

What joy; my heart is filled with love.
I am at a loss for words. How do I describe this wonderful feeling?
All I can say is thank you for showing me the way.
I now know this is my purpose; have you found yours?

Reincarnate To Try Again

Not long to go, just a little while longer. During my final minutes, I wonder: do I believe in reincarnation, can my soul really enter a new body and start a new life?

If so, could this be my comfort blanket, giving me peace of mind in case I made a hash of this life? I could then have another crack of the whip in the next one.

If I knew for sure there is life beyond this one, would it relieve the unbearable grief I am faced with after the death of a loved one? Would I then be able to deal with my heartache more easily and spend more time remembering the wonderful life they had; the joy of being in their presence, the fun, the laughter?

Perhaps then I would not be so terrified to let another person into my life to love again as it would not feel like an invitation for more pain.

After death is it our choice to remain in spirit form or return to flesh? How long do we have to decide? It is believed time does not exist in the spirit world; it is only relevant to us in the here and now.

If we have lived before, how long have we been around previously? We know this life is important for learning and developing, is that the same for all our lives?

Where do I go next? What do I do with all this wisdom I have accumulated? Do I return to earth to correct my mistakes, or do I stay in the spiritual realm and face my creator to answer the many questions for my action? Or could it be I who am judge and jury?

I am slipping away; this is my last day, my last hour, my last moment. Will I return? I will let you know.

(reincarnate photo) - by ccarlstead

Revenge is Not Always Sweet

I feel the need for justice; I should be able to take the law into my own hands as I was jilted.

I feel so angry, and sad; frustrated and vengeful.

This pain I feel is unbearable, surely my revenge is warranted? I know I shouldn't bury my aching heart, what else can I do other than rebel?

Many could say the person who hurt me just isn't worth the effort, but what do I do with the pain that eats away inside? It has spread all over my body, infecting every cell.

They are still in command of my life, even now after they are gone. The victory is theirs, for I am still suffering; their power still has a hold.

The damaged person is me; they however, are still intact. With no tatters or tears in sight they have no scars, no wounds to heal, nothing has harmed them. They are in control, or are they? I need to be strong to say goodbye. I need to forget this unhappy part of my life to allow space for the future wholesome times ahead. If I cling on to these unhealthy thoughts it can only drag me further down to the pit of despair.

If my departed lover sees me thriving in spite of the pain, this can only be the poetic justice I deserve. It is enough just to know my life is good now. I can see a future, without them inflicting further pain?

Release the baggage; holding on to negative emotions is an invitation for disease to creep in and have an influence on my health and wellbeing.

Learn from past mistakes, and never let a manipulative person rule my life again.

A relationship should enrich my life and make me happy. Now, I have my life back, my eyes are facing forward, the clouds are behind me and there they will remain.

(revenge photo) - by polina sergeeva

Rules and Regulations

Rules, rules, rules. Are these rules and regulations here to be broken? To live by rules gives clarity; we know the boundaries, and if we cross the boundary line we have to suffer the consequences.

Having an abundance of free-will, allows the devil into our lives; evil loves free-will; the wicked one will set a snare at every opportunity to try and influence every step we take.

He may disguise himself as a friend; someone I feel I can trust and rely on, someone who is loved and admired by all.

He may influence the vulnerable and guide them down a pathway of destruction, then groom them to believe his way is the only way.

There are some that have been engulfed with hatred and believe that certain religions are evil. Others are extremist followers of religion and believe their way is the only way to live; anything outside their belief is evil and must be destroyed. How can this be right? Their distorted views are destroying so many good, and innocent people.

Pray that evil is rejected, pray that good will ultimately shine through.

We have been given free will but still, we should abide by the rules.

If life isn't as good as we hoped, it is of our own making.

God, like my father, is there as a guide only. He is not there to live my life and control every minute of every day, that is for me to do.

So I cannot blame anyone else for the hardship I have experienced. I have taken this path and now I have to deal with it.

Sadness the Overwhelming Ache

I feel the muscles in my throat begin to tighten, and then liquid begins to slowly trickle from my eyes. This continues and increases until I feel as though all moisture has left my body. I try to regain my composure but each time I try, I feel I do not have control of my body. I shake all over, and break down again. The unfortunate, sometimes unexpected sorrow that overwhelms me and possesses every inch of my body is one of the most challenging of times. How do I cope with such pain?

When I was younger, I was not taught how to deal with these difficult times.

No matter how much my heart is broken, the world doesn't stop for my grief; it is only me that feels my grief.

As a child, my parents wanted to shield me from sadness, but has this caused further pain for me, as I do not know how to cope with certain difficult chapters in my life? Could this have increased the level of grief I feel, as it was such a shock to my system the first time I was faced with real grief? I felt like I was hit with a bullet that penetrated my heart; I didn't have the shielding cloak of my parents to protect me anymore.

Life can be overwhelming; grief never completely leaves us, it just eases as time moves forward.

It is good to remember I am given a choice every day, whether to allow sadness to rule my life, or find some peace from within.

Bring the sunshine back into my life once more; allow me to smile again.

Seize the day, and never have regrets.

Secrets Now Torment Later

If you do not share your secrets, you will live in fear of them; they will haunt you and stop you finding peace.

Secrets can damage your soul; the devil of deceit will grow inside. Do you really think you are hiding your secret from others?

We have all had secrets of some sort throughout our lives. Have you ever thought how lonely we are with secrets? The angel of honesty will defeat the devil of deceit, so be warned. The truth will surface one day.

Difficult times start to materialise; some are easy to overcome, some not so easy, and when the truth emerges it is too late; the damage is done. Have you been hiding behind the devil of deceit? He has taken a hold, and so you begin to fall apart as the angel of honesty fades.

Your tummy is in knots, your heart is shattered. You have lied to the ones you love, can forgiveness ever be found? Your actions were applauded by the devil and now you have to pay the price, for you ignored the angel of honesty.

If you are lucky enough to hide your secrets throughout your lifetime don't be fooled; you will never be able to continue your deceit when you are standing in front of your maker.

Why not cleanse your soul and right your wrongs before it is too late. You may think that God doesn't exist, but what if you are wrong? Are you willing to take the chance?

Shadows Should Not be Left in the Dark

If I bury my unhappy thoughts, emotions and experiences, they will only come back with a vengeance. They will continue to pierce my soul until I have no protective shield left.

When these painful thoughts bubble up I should release them through the written word. I should write in my journal, all the tormenting feelings I have that churn around inside me, day after day, in such an unbearably agonizing manner. These vile, flashing, images have a nasty habit of leaping into my mind without any warning. They arrive like an express train, peak, and then slowly fade away without any rationalization. Sadly the residue remains and increases as each day passes.

For a long time I have lived with the thought that perfection would lead to happiness. I have struggled for many years to rid my life of sad memories in the hope that one day my life would be perfect which I felt was the ultimate happiness.

If only I could learn that the bad experiences can help me to grow, then my life would be peaceful.

Acceptance is the first step to reducing my pain. I should embrace the negative emotions and treat them as experiences. They are blessings given to help me to grow; to create the finest life I can and to enjoy myself along the way.

My soul just 'is'. It is there to walk along in my shadow to remember the happy and sad times; both are opportunities to develop and learn. Leave the dark shadows behind as I progress; surrender my ego and let my inner soul be the driver. This is the true me without the influence of the venomous dark side. Embrace the silver lining when it arrives; this is what my soul intended.

Sleep – If Only I Could

I am grateful if I have not woken before the chimes of my bedside clock, for I know then I have slept all night. Sadly tonight is not one of those times. The clock beside my bed shows it is only thirty minutes past two in the morning; still many hours until the alarm is due to awaken me.

The sleepless nights are now repeating themselves on a daily basis, how can I stop this continuing cycle? I know some people can exist on just a few hours sleep; sadly I am in need of a full eight hours; any less and I do not feel refreshed or rested.

After yet another uneasy dream I lay in bed awake once again. I am so desperate to get back to sleep but the more I try, the harder it becomes. I attempt to relax my mind by taking in a deep breath. I picture a relaxing scene of a beautiful white sandy beach, which kisses the glistening gentle waves of the turquoise ocean. Sadly, after a few minutes, my mind drifts away from these calming thoughts and reverts back to the worries I have about events taking place the very next day. Then I begin to relive the bad things that happened the previous day. Before I know it I begin to recall every unpleasant memory I have ever had. My mind races searching out every nook and cranny; ignoring any good experience or happy thought, just homing in on the bad stuff. Each time I try and manoeuvre my mind back to something more pleasing I slip straight back to the disturbing ones.

Surely I should have control of my mind, but it feels like it has control of me. I wonder if my subconscious is in control? Perhaps it is a way to help me heal buried negative emotions. Should I listen to what appears to be unhelpful thoughts; they could be messages with a strong motive to heal the hurt inside? I close my eyes and let my mind drift to where it wants to go, accept, and welcome the healing to begin.

Soap Box

The country I live in is not the one I recognise anymore.

Many people believe our government is riddled with cowards, scared to step outside their stereotyped box for fear of rejection.

It is frustrating to hear so many excuses when we ask why our homeland is in such disorder. They seem to ignore the influx of asylum seekers who more often than not steal jobs from our young folk who could otherwise be receiving an apprenticeship with a local tradesman.

We then have the law enforcement officers who have their hands tied. If they put one foot wrong it results in disciplinary action. The thugs in the community play on their weakness, broadcasting their rights, and acting as if the world owes them something. How can order be restored when these 'hoodies' rule our streets?

Numerous hometowns have become similar to scenes in Third World countries. Full of garbage, graffiti everywhere, smashed shop windows; some areas show signs of drug abuse, with discarded syringes in the gutters.

No decent human being is able to walk in certain inner city areas for fear they may exit in a body bag.

Where is our pride? Will it ever return or has it disappeared forever?

Are we facing a revolution where there is no happy ending? Are the dark forces taking control, gushing through the veins of their vulnerable, but willing victims? Will my firm stance on my soapbox have any impact? Will anyone listen?

Let us stand side by side and fight for justice. Have faith that peace can be restored and harmony will blossom. Your help is needed to save our heritage now, for tomorrow could be too late.

(soap box photo) - by cgp grey

Soap Operas

Every day as I watch the turning hands of the clock I am nearer to my favourite time of the day. This is when I can live in my fantasy world; a time when I can disappear, leaving my troubles behind, into the world of soap operas.

For the next thirty minutes I am able to live in another world, one of drama, passion and heartache.

There is always intrigue and excitement, and often unbelievable adventures. It surprises me how the characters generally bounce back after surviving their ordeal. Their bravery is something I envy as by the time the next episode is due to air, they are back and fighting fit; often after escaping a near death experience. Their sobbing has completely ceased and their black hole of despair has vanished.

Why do I crave these television shows? Do the lives of the cast members appear more interesting than mine? They seem to deal with problems so well. But I wonder; do they have more emotional strength? I want to mould my life so I live as they do. But wait; do I need to rely on others to have this strength?

I am here for a reason; I just wish I knew what destiny has in store. However much I admire the television soap opera characters, this is not reality.

My life is reality so I should enjoy every moment, otherwise I will just be wasting my life.

Time is precious, it can never be reclaimed; don't waste it.

So So Stubborn

I understand stubbornness is a form of selfishness whether it is for good or bad reasons.

I know I can be stubborn at times, but I should try and conclude any disagreement with a peaceful outcome and sever any remaining, unhealthy, feelings that are directed at others.

I know my stubbornness can become a barrier for my personal development if I allow it. Is it not an advantage, to allow my stubborn streak to be noticed?

A top class athlete has to be stubborn to achieve perfection to cross the finish line first. A chief executive has to be stubborn because he needs the perseverance and drive to be able to continue fighting on even when the going is tough. Sometimes stubbornness can be an advantage and so any feelings of guilt can be discarded.

How do I deal with the inflexibility of others? When the arguments arise, then the constant battle of wills to persuade each other their way is the right way.

There are times I want my own way; I often know inside that the other person is right, but still, I do everything in my power to fight on so I get what I want. I just don't like the idea of being wrong. My defence mechanism kicks in, then my ego takes control, and I pity anyone who gets in my way.

The potential damage can arise when I don't want to admit that I'm wrong so an apology is out of the question. Will this cause more pain than if I swallow my pride? If I let this stubbornness continue I could lose the ones I love.

Perhaps I can gain empowerment by realising that saying sorry is not a weakness but strength. If I give it a try to see what happens it may not be that bad. Perhaps even make me feel good and bring about a peaceful agreement that is satisfying for all. Worth a shot don't you think?

(so so stubborn photo) - by labella vida

Sorry for Being Sorry

I'm sorry I so often feel the need to say I'm sorry. It is true; the ones I care for are the ones I hurt the most. I know if I try and conceal my bad behaviour it will only increase the hurt you feel. The damage will be amplified if I try to camouflage my blunder.

My mistake has always been to cover up my blunders, this sin added to sin, adds to more sin. I have ruined my apologies in the past with defensive excuses. No resolution can be reached until I stop defending my words and actions.

It's not easy to undo the hurt I have caused you; perhaps time will help heal and maybe you can forgive me.

I know your mercy will not alter the past hurts, but it can clear our path for a brighter future.

Many tears I have shed; how I wish I could turn back the clock for now I know how much hurt I have caused you. Your pain in my pain, I feel so desperate inside.

My one error is being human, and this can be my downfall, for humans are prone to making mistakes. Perfection can only be achieved once in a while. More often than not my life runs along at an average speed. But sadly, I occasionally let go of my true self which allows the horrible side of me to take control. Regrettably this is the price I pay for being human. I am just a complete mix of good and bad.

I'm sorry for hurting you and I'm sorry I made you cry. I said many things I did not mean and am left with many regrets. Do not let the error of my ways be a tragic end to the wonderful bond we have. Please forgive me for being a fool, for I am only human after all.

(sorry photo) - by dunikowski

Spiritual Warfare

I should not be fearful of the spirit world, especially the lower world energies. There are more unsavoury people on this earth than in the spirit world.

If I listen to the demon spirits around me they will remind me that my false self is riddled with uneasiness for they know fear is just beneath the surface. Before long it will cause all happiness to vanish; I will be smothered with sadness as my fear increases, anger, hatred and rage will multiply.

I need the wise guidance from our divine creator to envelop me with a wonderful protective shining cloak made from pure love, peace and harmony. This will keep me safe and secure and I will have trust that good ultimately always wins through.

I must never listen to the demon spirit; it will fill me with anger and hatred.

Life can throws obstacles along my path; so I am then faced with a slippery downward slope, followed by a ragged rocky uphill climbs. When I am feeling low and my guard is down, I am constantly having internal wars; the demon spirit tries to creep in and cloud my judgement, tempting me towards their wicked sinful ways.

Evil will triumph if righteousness does nothing. If you, like me, are just starting out on your spiritual path, ask for guidance from above. This will help heal any negative blocks and fears and so you can begin your journey with a clear head and open heart.

I know love is the strongest emotion, we must only listen to honest love, but be careful evil can also feel love. It loves hardship, sadness and anger; it is delighted when we argue with others, and it laughs when we cry. So don't be fooled; love does not always come in the form of good. Make sure the gift of love you receive is pure.

Bless you and good luck.

(spiritual photo) - by black locust

Sub-Human – I Think Not!

I loathe being surrounded by so many people; it only compounds my feeling of isolation. I have never felt part of anything, my family, my school, or my work.

I preferred to be alone; I just didn't seem to fit in anywhere.

Sadly this originated from an early age. I was bullied at school, often told I was not even worthy of being part of the human race. My anger grew as a result and for a while I became defensive and aggressive. It took control of my life. Thankfully the defensiveness passed, as I grew older and wiser.

As time passed, my life was just like any other kid in our neighbourhood. I went to school and studied well. After many years of education I departed with an honours degree, so why do I still feel I am not worthy and beneath all others around me?

Some may feel their skin colour puts them at a disadvantage, and only Caucasians can be privileged. I am Caucasian so why then am I treated as though I am sub-human. Could it be because I am a woman?

The next time you feel the need to be cruel to a fellow human being, take a moment to reflect on my words. I have suffered by the hands and words of man since I was a child, as have many women over the centuries. Thankfully, my life is now settled and I know I am equal to all. Take heed of my words, for the dark ages are in the past.

I am not beneath you, I am not your slave; I am just as good as you. Let's be gracious enough to respect and embrace each other's strengths and weaknesses, to live along-side each other harmoniously.

(subhuman photo) - by faronwille

Tears that Flow

When the floodgates open, how do I regain my composure? Sometimes emotions just flow and however much I try, there is no end in sight. When my mind allows me to take a rest from the raw emotional pain, should I remain cocooned from the world to avoid potential questions about my outburst? I'm sure it would lead to discussions I would prefer not to have, as I know I am liable to break down again? How would I cope in front of an audience? Will I be able to speak, or will I stutter and stammer? Can I hold back the tears or will I crumble and fall? Will I begin to tremble, and if I do, will the trembles fester? Will they be stored inside until one day, when I am least expecting it, the explosion occurs when I will fall apart and mentally breakdown into tiny little fragments as the pain has been left to fester for so long.

It feels like every part of my body aches; every emotion is stretched to its limit. Do I have a choice? Do I really hold the key? Will I let the rumblings flow and deal with the nagging twinge now? Or shall I wait for the eruption and deal with the stored pain that, once opened, will turn into a tsunami; out of control and sure to cause devastation.

I know eventually the tidal wave will calm. Once it has found its level, and the furious flow has diminished, peace will return and perhaps clarity will show me the way ahead. Maybe then I will have the vision of trust and belief in myself to find the strength to move forward, with ease, to the brighter days ahead.

(tears photo) - by lau_lau chan

Techno-Junkie

My life is filled with gadgets. Every corner of every room in my home and workplace is bursting with the latest devices. My pleasure lasts a short time as I enjoy my delightful new possession. Then, sadly, a couple of weeks later a new model is released and appears on the shelves.

I am always so desperate to have modern gizmos, even if they are almost identical to my existing ones. I can't help myself; hey-presto there I go again, the compulsive buying process begins once more.

Is there something missing in my life? Perhaps this is why I am so obsessed with trying to fill a void with my shiny new material objects. Perhaps I am just greedy? I never really appreciate my possessions; once I have parted with my cash and they have taken up residence in my home they become meaningless.

I am never content, I just want more. Then again, do I just want to keep up-to-date with technology? Surely this is a good thing, after all it is forward thinking.

I try to imagine how life would have been without these wonderful gadgets. I couldn't live without my computer; my mobile phone is permanently by my side. How did our ancestors survive?

If I have a question it can instantly be resolved. I simply type away, and then within seconds, my computer has given the answer to my question. No matter how strange my query, there is someone with a solution, or just a new idea.

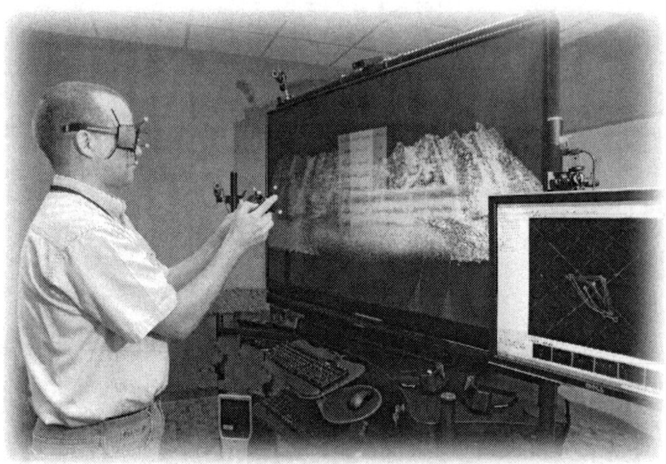

So many have given their time to offer us all an explanation, it has made the world a smaller place.

We can now stretch out far and wide at the press of a button, and share with others this joyous time. Our wonderful new technological age is here, and here to stay.

(techno junkie photo) - by idaho national laboratory

Thorn in My Side

Who is the thorn in my side? Could it be you? Would you ever be aware if it were you? Would you ever feel you could be the cause of the sharp piercing feeling I have in my heart? Surely if you did you would change your ways, wouldn't you? Does it really please you to hurt others? How can this be? How cruel can you be to smile at another's pain and anguish?

If I were to remove the thorn, would my wound ever heal or would the spikes of the thorn scar me for life?

Could I find a way to smile again, or have the years of sadness permanently turned down the outer corners of my mouth? Do I have to live with this expression of sadness and bitterness?
We have all met people well known for their grumpiness; were they always this way? Could they have been yet another victim of somebody's piercing thorn?

Should this be our lesson? Never judge someone at first glance? If you can, look beyond the scars, some are more obvious than others. Look deep into the eyes of the victim, as they never lie; wait to see the story unfold.
As for me, will my happiness return? I should cut the cord to anyone who is having a negative influence on my life. I should not have to suffer anymore. I sit, I wonder, and I wait for the right moment.

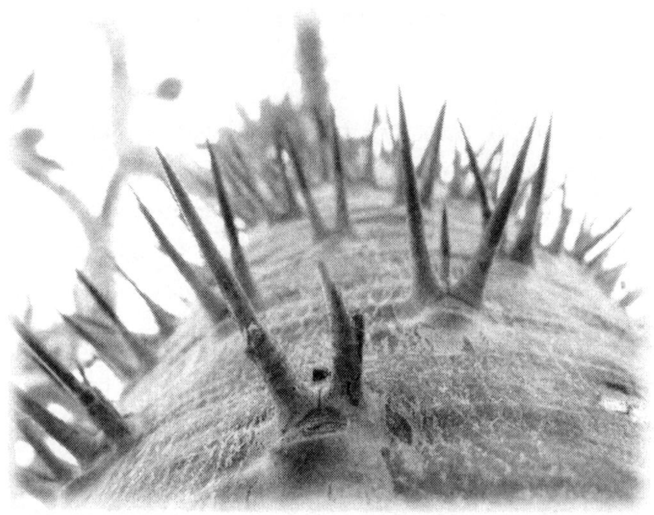

I will make my move today. Give me the strength and confidence to grasp every layer of buried negative emotion, and release it so I can have the power to face the day ahead.

(thorn in my side photo) - by orin zebest

Toxic Emotions

If you poison your soul with toxic emotions, your family's lives will be tainted, troubled till the end; the same time hindering any relationship you desire with God. Those evil, toxic, emotions sometimes rear their ugly heads to contaminate our lives.

Shameful acts result in painful emotions. Depression, guilt, anger and fear, all pollute our lives.

Who sends these harmful emotions that can destroy the strongest of us all? How can we rid ourselves of these damaging toxic emotions? Shame cannot remain in the shadows; the darkness can only conceal pain for a while. The longer it is left, the more it will fester and infect our soul.

Toxic emotions are buried alive; the pain is only numbed not banished, and it can never be cremated until justice is served.

Shame will never allow you to have a deep and trusting relationship; you will not be as one with God, your partner or your family. Negative emotions try to shut out the pain, and hope nobody notices.

To begin the healing process be honest and have faith in yourself. Healing your soul is like peeling an onion. Layer-by-layer you uncover more toxic emotions until you reach the main core where freedom can be found. As the darkness fades, allow the light to shine.

Keep it shining, and if the 'emotional onion' tries to develop again, take a moment to reflect and remember the heartache you felt. Once again, slowly begin to peel away the skin of the onion, and rejoice in your newfound freedom.

(toxic emotions photo) - by adobe of chaos

Utopia For All if You Try

Was the Garden of Eden the ultimate Utopia until Adam and Eve were lead astray by Satan's serpent? Can I ever find Utopia within? Does it exist for me? Or, as I turn each corner, am I destined to live my life with this continuing suffering and heartache?

I want to live in my fantasy Utopia, my imaginary perfect world. Does this mean I really don't have free will, for if I did I wouldn't chose to live this way, feeling that my struggles are never ending?

I worry about money; will I ever feel I am in control of my finances? My health is suffering, I'm sure it's because I am worrying so much.

I dream at night of Utopia, that wonderful, peaceful, tranquil place, filled with smiling faces. There is an abundance of food and nobody is suffering through ill health.

As I dream my dream, I am filled with warmth; my whole body is rejoicing in this incredible feeling. As I stir, the sensation begins to fade; the more I become conscious, the more the memory diminishes; don't go, don't go, stay with me.

I struggle to stay asleep to remain in my magnificent fantasy world. Sadly the sorrow returns, bringing back the dark gloomy clouds, for another day.

To fight away the cloud feels like a challenging task, almost impossible, as it darkens my world, dampens my spirit and chills me raw through to my bones.

To find the warmth needed to fight and ultimately unearth my Utopia, I must locate the fire within; burn away the clouds, and rejoice in my Utopia.

Worry Will Keep you Hostage

Worry robs us of the present. It is like a steam train racing along the track; before we know it, life has passed us by.

What is worrying you today? Do you really think worry keeps you safe?

Do not let worry hold you hostage. What is it that really worries you, commands control over you? Visualise your worry as a movie. You could have the ability to press the fast forward button to reach the end sooner and so stop the worrying dragging on.
You could also reduce the size of the movie which in-turn reduces the worry until eventually it will disappear.

Sometimes you may have to accept that the only way to gain peace and harmony is to cut the connection cords to the person who is having a negative influence on you. If all they do is bring dark clouds into your life then gently walk away and conceal your tracks so your pathway cannot be followed. The negative person can no longer walk along the same route as you.

Does your worry make you feel ashamed? If you have excess weight perhaps you even worry how your partner could desire you? Do you continually try to cover up the unsightly bulges, the love handles, and the flabby skin under the arms?

The orange-peel looking cellulite is so horrible to view in the mirror; who could be attracted to such a huge lump of lard? Could you be worrying for no reason? Ask yourself the question; has your partner refused your advances in the bedroom recently, turned down the opportunity for a night of passion, or do they count their lucky stars they have scored? The only person who cringes at the sight of your reflection is you.

Worry does not resolve the problem; it merely clouds your mind, increases negative emotions, and drains your body and mind of happiness.

Love yourself a little today and a little more tomorrow; it will honestly all be worth it.

Wrinkles

Wrinkles are leftovers from smiles. Never feel sad about wrinkles, as without a lot of smiles, wrinkles would never appear.

I love to laugh and enjoy myself, and so what is more important, to look miserable without a single wrinkle, or have many laughter lines and a beaming happy smile?

I only look in the mirror for a short while, in the morning and at night. The rest of my time is spent looking at the world around me. Why should I be so concerned with my looks and how I appear to everyone else? If I don't have to put up with looking at my reflection for long, why do I continually worry about my appearance? In fact I think I should feel proud of my wrinkles. They have matured with me, they belong to me. They are an indication of how my experiences, both good and bad, have shaped my life.

I am familiar with each one. I know when the first one appeared, and I remember what I was doing in my life at that time.

My wrinkles were once my enemy. I used to waste many moments thinking about how I hated them; now they are my friends. I no longer feel uncomfortable with the way I look. It is a pleasure to have many experiences and so many stories to tell.

Do I really want to be a beautiful person outside without having an equally beautiful soul inside?

Inner beauty will shine through, as this is what makes life worth living.

(wrinkles photo) - by andrewr

Yesterday

Be happy today, as yesterday will never happen again. Do not be glum; for what is done is done and will remain unchangeable. The sleepless nights, the anxious days, cannot be changed; there is no second chance to live yesterday again.

Yesterday belonged to you, every minute, every hour. It may not all have been good or enjoyable or worthwhile, but still it was all yours. Don't wait for tomorrow to make that important call to your best friend just to say hello; delaying could be heart breaking, because tomorrow may never come for them. Our yesterdays hold some magical memories, some filled with joy and laughter. We try to copy this for tomorrow, but sometimes it never happens.

Many years can be wasted, and some we may wish to forget. Some memories are there to be cherished, and some we may wish to bury; but from all of them we learn, as they are our yesterdays.

Make all your yesterdays, today's, and tomorrows purposeful. Your memories will be stored away for contemplation later, if needed.

Today is for living so enjoy.

(yesterday photo) - by aunt omree